i heard a crow before i was born

Also by Jules Delorme

Ahshiá:ton: You Should Write It (short stories)

Faller (poetry)

i heard
a crow before
i was born

jules delorme

GOOSE LANE

Edited by Jazz Cook.
Cover and page design by Julie Scriver.
Cover image copyright © 2024 by Jennifer Deschamps.
Printed in Canada by Marquis.
10 9 8 7 6 5 4 3 2 1

Library and Archives Canada Cataloguing in Publication

Title: i heard a crow before i was born / Jules Delorme.
Names: Delorme, Jules, author.
Identifiers: Canadiana (print) 20240355245 | Canadiana (ebook) 2024035527X | ISBN
9781773104089 (softcover) | ISBN 9781773104096 (EPUB)
Subjects: LCSH: Delorme, Jules. | LCSH: Generational trauma. | CSH: First
Nations—Residential schools. | CSH: Kanyen'kehà:ka—Ethnic identity. | CSH:
Kanyen'kehà:ka—Biography. | LCGFT: Autobiographies.
Classification: LCC E99.M8 D45 2024 | DDC 305.897/55420092—dc23

Goose Lane Editions acknowledges the generous support of the Government of
Canada, the Canada Council for the Arts, and the Government of New Brunswick.

Goose Lane Editions is located on the unceded territory of the Wəlastəkwiyik whose
ancestors along with the Mi'kmaq and Peskotomuhkati Nations signed Peace and
Friendship Treaties with the British Crown in the 1700s.

Goose Lane Editions
500 Beaverbrook Court, Suite 330
Fredericton, New Brunswick
CANADA E3B 5X4
gooselane.com

There have been so many heroes in my life that I cannot name them all. Some of them are spoken about here. What they all taught me, even those who are not mentioned, and what I was slow to learn, is that courage is not being willing to die. It is having the will and the fortitude to live.

Contents

i heard a crow before i was born

i heard a crow before i was born.

i heard tsó:ka'we before i was born.

it was dark and wet and warm in a way that i will never know again and i heard a crow call out.

a lone tsó:ka'we.

even then i knew that the loneliest sound on earth is a crow calling out and there being no answer. that crows are among the most social birds and a tsó:ka'we being alone is a tragedy that echoes through nature and beyond.

tsó:ka'we is a trickster in kanien'kehá:ka in mohawk culture. the people of jack the man who called himself my father but i would never call father but most importantly my tóta my grandmother and her beliefs because it was she that mattered most. not because it matters in kanien'kehá:ka law the female not the male line and female not the male clan but because it was she who gave me reason to stay alive when my life was the deepest darkest and bloodiest and it seemed there was nothing to live for and no one neither of my parents and no one else in my family wanted me but she my tóta treasured me and taught me the old kanien'kehá:ka ways and told me stories and told me of the tricksters tsó:ka'we and nikakwaho'tà:'a coyote and tehahonhtané:ken rabbit. those tricksters were always up to no good and whenever i heard a tsó:ka'we i knew that if she was not calling to her mate she was laughing and very likely laughing at me.

i have always been fond of tsó:ka'we and her laughter and her tricks.

but there is a call that tsó:ka'we makes a cry out to her mate a cry out to any other crow that still breaks my heart.

for whatever reason jack's violence towards my mother escalated when she was pregnant with me. i don't know if he beat her when she was pregnant with my older sister debby. he probably did. but he got really violent with her when she was pregnant with me. at one point he dragged her down the stairs by her hair and stomped up and down on her belly.

i learned about this later in letters she wrote and then from my step father my real father dalton the only man i called father dalton the white man who stayed and tried to love my mother's children even though we made ourselves so hard to love but i knew before then about the beating when i was in my mother's womb because i felt it.

because i felt it.

in my darkness that heat and darkness that i would never know again i felt the blows and his voice like a dim roar from out there.

it was as if he hated me even before i was born.

it was as if he was trying to kill me even before i was born.

no. not as if. he hated me and he tried to kill me before i was born.

jack would never call himself mohawk. he would never call himself kanien'kehá:ka. he would never have used either of those words. this was the 1960s and while it was obvious he was indian that's what they called it then you did everything you could to forget what you were and where you were from and so, like the father he seemed to despise so much, he often tried to pass himself off as french and with the name and his ability to speak french he fooled some people. not all but some.

maybe that's why he was so angry.

particularly at my mother who was white and was french though she was of irish descent.

before i was born she left him for my step father my real father while jack was in prison.

she gave birth to me in a barn feeding the pigs when she was visiting a friend just outside of toronto. there was a crow in the rafters.

she was very quiet as she watched me being born. she did not cry out. my mother knew pain and she knew how to take pain in silence. tsó:ka'we knew about the beatings when she called to me and tsó:ka'we was telling me that life would play many tricks on me and i would survive and i would know love and even know some laughter.

or at least that is what i think she was saying.

i struggle at times to speak tsó:ka'we.

i have felt connection to many animals throughout my life. more animals than people. dogs. horses. goats. bears. particularly bears. particularly ohkwá:ri. my grandmother my tóta was a clan mother of the ohkwá:ri as well a practitioner of medicine. but the tricksters. oh the tricksters. to hear tsó:ka'we because she likes to laugh and make noise my heart and my spirit feel lighter.

maybe i answered tsó:ka'we.

maybe in my mother's womb i answered tsó:ka'we's call.

maybe that's why my jack hated me.

maybe he thought my mother was giving birth to a trickster.

i do not know.

i have never felt like a trickster.

i like to laugh and i like to play jokes. but i was an abnormally quiet and serious child diagnosed as autistic later as asperger's that's what they called it then and dyslexic and very very angry. i fought a lot. always bigger boys or gangs of boys. maybe i was trying to get them to kill me. the only time i laughed as a child was with animals.

i became more playful as i got older once i moved away from the reserve from cornwall and i learned to love the tricksters but i never counted myself as one of them.

i love mischief even then but i did not think of myself as a trickster.

not when i was young.

i was too young. too busy fighting and screaming and gnashing. i was not cultivating the aspect of an angry young man. aside from my violent past my asperger's made me very intense and obsessive and antisocial. there was nothing then that was playful about me.

but i heard tsó:ka'we call me when i was born.

i knew that meant something.

i know that means something.

tsó:ka'we did not call to me without reason.

i heard her.

i heard the trickster call to me before i was born.

i heard tsó:ka'we call to me before i was born.

ohkwá:ri

i met an ohkwá:ri a bear once many years ago in the woods.

a big grizzly bear.

that was as close to seeing god as i would ever come. i don't know why he didn't kill me. maybe he was full. maybe it wasn't my day to die. maybe i was too small to eat. i was only seven or eight years old.

i was in the british columbia woods my uncles and my father were part of a group that travelled during hunting seasons all over canada to various reserves to hunt and trap with various tribes and in various places or they would come to our reserve to hunt with us it was some kind of unofficial project that someone just started up. very typically indian that's what we called it then. let's go here. okay. simple as that.

i would join a group of boys some from my reserve and others more local mostly older than me although i in my arrogance thought that of course i was the wisest hunter who also went hunting. we rarely caught anything but we imagined ourselves as great ancient hunters who knew all the secrets because it was in our blood. my uncles and my friend roger an older boy from my reserve had begun to teach me how to hunt but i was only seven or eight and i had an old hand me down twenty two winchester that jammed more than it shot. so while i thought of myself as a hunter i was no expert and most of the other boys were older so they were not inclined to listen to what i considered my great wisdom. being the already proud and stubborn and angry boy that i was made me very angry and so i stomped off by myself into woods i did not know.

i was a foolish boy who grew into an even more foolish man.

there i was stomping through the woods with my rusty twenty two thrown over my shoulder. i was stomping across a shallow stream brooding and pouting when i stopped dead.

this was my habit as is still my habit. my head was down and i sensed something. stop and listen. roger had taught me that too.

i knew something was wrong. maybe it was the smell or maybe he made a sound but i knew he was there before i looked up.

it probably saved my life. i often forget that lesson as we do so many of our most valuable lessons but at that moment i did the right thing and it almost certainly saved my life. i was walking almost directly towards the grizzly bear he was only a few feet away and looking right at me and he probably would have swatted me out of reflex. a single swat from such a massive and incredibly powerful being would have either killed me at once or left me so wrecked that i would have died in those woods.

i knew at that moment that i was dead.

the rifle was on my shoulder but even if it fired it was a twenty two and it would only annoy him. i had no chance of killing him. his breath reeked. i can only begin to describe some of the smell. a combination of rotting meat fish and something else something that i would now describe only as death. many other things. none of them good.

he was enormous.

gigantic.

the most massive living beast that i'd ever encountered.

compared to my little boy's body i can only begin to convey how massive he seemed to me. how massive he was. the mightiest thing that i'd ever encountered. the mightiest thing that i have yet to encounter up that close.

i stared at him.

he stared at me.

i knew he was a male right away because of his size and the massive hump on his back. i'd seen a grizzly female and her pups from a distance and had been told by my uncles how to tell them apart. i also knew he was a male from all of the scars on his face and his body. females rarely fight each other. only males feel the need to prove themselves by fighting each other. bears are no different than humans in that way. this one was old enough and rough enough that he had obviously been in many fights.

i never even considered using my rifle. i was a puny human and he was an ohkwá:ri the mightiest of the ohkwá:ri. this far south he was the mightiest thing in this forest the mightiest thing that i would ever be this close to in my life.

i was at his mercy.

i was at his very whim.

perhaps it was knowing this and perhaps it was accepting this that put my young usually fervent and angry mind at peace.

for just that moment i was completely at peace.

he looked at me.

he had been drinking at the stream i think because his head was low and his mouth was open. water still dripped from his mouth.

i could not even begin to comprehend to even begin to grasp how massive and all powerful the bear was.

i had never seen so large so massive and mighty a head. i imagined a sledgehammer would not break it.

we stared at each other for what seemed like an eternity but was probably only a matter of seconds.

we just stared. neither of us moved. his eyes his huge brown eyes were not the eyes of a mere creature of flesh and blood but conveyed the assumption of being all powerful that only a god might have.

and then the ohkwá:ri huffed a great big huff that actually created a wind not a twinkling breeze but a mighty wind upon my face and he turned and walked into the woods.

i stood there for a while longer.

in silence.

in absolute awe.

transfixed.

i'm not sure how long i stood there.

maybe minutes.

maybe hours.

meeting that bear that ohkwá:ri was as close and remains as close as i have ever come to a truly religious experience.

i had encountered a god. a living god.

i stood there in the awe of that experience for a while. i don't know for how long.

i have a thing. i never get lost in the wilderness even if i it is a wilderness i do not know. i don't know how i do it. i get lost in areas of the city that i've lived in for years. but i never get lost in the wilderness. i found my way back to the village and i didn't mention the bear the ohkwá:ri. it was too sacred to speak.

i have never forgotten that bear. that ohkwá:ri.

i will never forget him.

he was as close to a god as i will ever come.

that ohkwá:ri.

that grizzly bear.

i don't know why he let me live.

that ohkwá:ri.

that grizzly bear.

but he will live.

as long as i live.

i met a god that day.

an honest to goodness god.

i know what a god looks like.

i know what meeting a god feels like.

for me it will always be that bear.

for me it will always be that moment with that mighty ohkwá:ri.

that god.

that bear.

that ohkwá:ri.

he always hit me in the head

he always hit me in the head.

mostly in the back of my head.

he liked to kick me when i was down too but after they took me to see people at cornwall general hospital and they tested my i.q. and it was 152. they told my mother it was 8 points less than einstein's though he was never actually tested. einstein that is. she took me because a catholic school teacher wanted to put me in retarded school. that's what they called it then. that's what they called me then. retarded. a retarded little indian. a retarded little half breed. i would later be diagnosed with autism with asperger's and dyslexia but what mattered to my mother was that she had a son that was a genius. just like wile e. coyote. i thought it was a good thing because she was nice to me for a while after that. she didn't hit me or try to kill me for a while. she told everybody who would listen that her son was a genius because it had to come from her. jack was definitely no genius.

and of course that's exactly what she told jack when he came to take me back to the reserve.

and that's when he started hitting me in the head.

sometimes with his fists. with his big calloused fists. sometimes with his feet. sometimes with anything he could find anything he could pick up.

almost killed me a few times.

but it turns out i'm hard to kill. i like to joke that i'm harder to kill than a russian monk.

one time he hit me so hard with a cast iron frying pan that i went blind.

i don't know how long i went blind for. somehow i found my way into the woods and fell down into a hollow. i don't know if i lost consciousness. i don't know how much time actually passed. i don't know if the seizures started then or if i always had them. maybe it's just the story i tell myself. that if they didn't start then they got a lot worse.

so i can blame one more thing on him.

now i'm old. i'm on medication for the seizures but i still fall down and i pass out. not long ago i broke my arm reaching for a bowl of cherries on the top shelf of the fridge. i've been in more fights that i can count jumped out of planes in the army climbed mountains and caves did all kinds of crazy things but i've never done anything crazier than break my arm reaching for a bowl of cherries. i went down and my arm stayed up. i've broken pretty much every bone in my body but this one was so ridiculous that it still seems to hurt more than the others. mind you i broke my arm in two places one being at the elbow. my arm looked like something from a horror movie.

i had learned to live without possessions when living with jack on the reservation. he was given to selling what he could and destroying what he couldn't during his drunken rages. and he would disappear for long periods of time. i don't remember if he told me and others he was in prison or if i just assumed. and though he was in prison often there was another reason that i would not find out about later. it meant i got left alone a lot to fend for myself from a very young age.

i got made fun of by other kids and was the object of disgust by even the adults of the reserve and the housing projects because i wore the same dirty clothes and my shoes were often falling apart and filthy. i was that poor kid that other poor kids made fun of for being so poor. charity workers and even some relatives would give me clothes usually hand me downs but jack or my mother would destroy them or throw them in the garbage. it would make them angry that strangers gave me things that they could not or did not give me.

anyway.

jack's mother my tóta my grandmother therese and my grandfather fernand met in residential school. i don't know what they were like then but by the time i came along they had taken very different paths in life. tóta went back to the traditional ways became a clan mother a medicine woman. she was kind. strong and kind. she loved me. she believed that my strangeness meant i had the medicine too and she taught me much about the old ways.

he fernand became a fanatic catholic who declared over and over that she was going to hell because she was a witch and he only spoke french so i barely understood him. i'm sure he spoke to me. he must have spoken to me. but i don't remember his voice and i only dimly remember his face. i remember that he tried to win me over to his side rather than hers. i was the oldest son of the oldest son. and so there was a war for my soul. i was supposed to be named after him and they made it my middle name but somebody somehow got it wrong on the birth certificate and it was spelled fernend and even though that's only one letter different it is still not the same name.

when he would walk into the room jack or my uncles and my aunts would leave the room. my tóta would not even speak to him. she would not say his name. i only understood later what those things meant. why jack was so angry why my aunts and uncles lived such miserable lives why my tóta would not even speak his name.

did jack's violence begin with fernand. today i think fernand created the monster that was my blood father but if fernand was born that way was i born with that monster inside me.

i spent my life trying to deny it trying to hide from it trying to turn away from it. but i have jack inside of me and i have my grandfather inside of me and i have my mother inside of me just like i have all the good people my tóta and my teachers and my friends inside of me and my ancestors the kanien'kehá:ka the mohawk that's an algonquin word that means maneater they called themselves kanien'kehá:ka which means people of the flint but they liked mohawk just fine because it scared people. one of my ancestors probably ate a priest. all of that is inside me too. but does that mean i have a monster inside me or was the monster created by other people.

what is it faulkner said like ripples in a pond and you were not even there to see the rock thrown and you begin to blame. but where do you i stop blaming. the residential schools. the priests. the settlers. the ancestors.

for years i blamed jack the man who called himself my father.

that was easy. that was obvious. he hit me. he beat me up. he hit me in the head. so did my mother. she even tried to kill me. but she was mentally ill so i couldn't blame her but i could blame my blood father who wasn't mentally ill. he was just mean. he was in control. he could decide. i could hate him and i did oh i did so much but now that i am old and broken down and even though much of the damage much of the seizures and the falling down and the memory loss and the pain in my head is almost certainly from his beatings i look back and i believe that he was only passing on what was done to him and maybe my grandfather was only passing on what was done to him and did it start there or before where does the blame start not that it absolves them but there has to be a why and a why before that and which is the first why though my blood father's people did not believe in the bible was there a cain and was there a why for cain and a why for adam and a why for eve where and why was the first angry blow struck. when did the hate start. where does the blame start and where does the blame stop.

i am still angry at jack.

i am still so angry at jack.

my anger grew as i learned more about what he went on to do. perhaps i am angry at myself because i know i carry that man that jack inside of me. i became like the pitbulls that were always in our yard on the reserve. i just went everywhere looking for a fight and when i found one i put my head down and charged. i began to like getting hit in the head. i picked fights with bigger and older boys and with groups and when we moved to toronto i picked fights with bullies. i became a fighter a professional fighter and then a professional trainer but my head was not built to take that much punishment. now i fall down. i have seizures. i have monumental pain. i have begun to forget things and i sometimes become confused about what i'm doing about who i am or where i am.

i learned to like getting hit in the head.

and i can say it all started because he liked to hit me in the head.

but is that where it started.

is that where the blame starts.

is that where jack's story starts.

is that where fernand's story starts.

is that where i start.

is it that simple.

am i that simple.

were you.

are you.

are you that simple jack.

you like to hit me in the head.

he liked to hit me in the head.

that's all i chose to know about him.

that's all i wanted to know about him.

he liked to hit me in the head.

and i learned to like being hit in the head.

and i've forgotten so much.

but this i know.

tóta

when i remember you my tóta my grandmother what i
remember is the kindness that you showed me and your
wisdom and the way your calloused hands felt on my cheek.
your name was therese but i never knew that while you were
alive. to me you were always and you will always be tóta.
you would call me over when i was angry which i very often
was or when i was freaking out about something or when i
just felt like giving up. you always seemed to know and you
would put both your calloused warm hands on my cheeks
and speak to me in that voice that coming from the back of
your throat voice that whenever i hear another indian that's
what they called it then speak that still warms me even just
the memory of your touch still warms me in a way that just
makes me glad to be alive even when i'm not. i think i go to
pow wows just to hear the sound of those voices because it
was often not what you said but the sound of that voice and
the feel of those hands on my cheeks which no one else has
ever done to me because i don't like to be touched but your
touch your touch so firm and so quiet and your voice literally
kept me alive.

sometimes i think i can still feel your touch and hear your
voice. sometimes i know that i can. sometimes i know that
you are here with me and the rage or the pain or the just
plain tired of living a life that never seemed to want me in
it gets lost and all there is are your hands and your voice.
and your smell. you smelled like sage and tobacco and the

burning plants of the smudge and the earth and cedar and forgiveness and kindness. and love.

you smelled like love to me.

you smell like love to me.

but i cannot picture your face in detail anymore.

you have become a blur to me.

a ghost.

a loving spirit.

i know you were not a small woman a skinny woman like my mother and that you had grey hair and that you sometimes wore glasses. but i cannot see you even in my dreams i only feel you sometimes like you are right there with me and i would be willing to live for those times alone no matter how much pain or sadness or hurt that i have to carry those moments when i feel you are all that really matters to me.

i knew you for so few years. so very few when compared to how long i've been alive. and yet you remain with me and sometimes you're all that i have but that is enough that is more than enough and when i feel your hands on my cheeks it is like medicine not pills and hospitals but the ancient medicine in which you believed the healing medicine that doesn't quite heal me. nothing can fully heal what i have lived but it reaches and warms my spirit in the way no modern medicine can and i feel i can go on even when i think that i can't i know that i can't go on i will go on because you touched me because you spoke to me because you loved me because you were there. because you were in my life. and that is enough that is more than enough.

you never spoke about your early life.

i know that you and fernand were products of the residential school and that while he tried to become as catholic and as french and as not indian as he could and jack too tried to become as french and as not indian though not a catholic jack detested catholics oh how jack detested catholics you came out and went back to traditional kanien'kehá:ka ways and that you became a clan mother and a medicine woman and people on the island respected you even revered you and some like fernand and my mother feared you and condemned you and said you were a witch and you and he fernand never spoke a word back and forth to each other that i remember though he often ranted at you especially when he was drunk you never answered back you never even acknowledged him though i heard you speak french the only language that he would speak.

but you spoke kanien'kehá:ka words to me and some english. i remember only a few kanien'kehá:ka words. i had to take a class and was one of the slowest students. when i think of that half of my heritage i do not think of jack or fernand i think of you and roger who taught me how to hunt and to be in the woods in the wild i think of your voice and your hands on my cheek and your smell and everything that was good. the only thing that was good about me as a child is forever painted by that memory of you and that if nothing else makes me more indian that's what we were called then than white no matter what anyone says or sees you are more a part of me and you are more with me than anyone or anything else and for that i do not know how to thank you because no words or gestures would ever be enough for what you were to me what you are to me what you will always be to me.

you are my tóta.

you are the very kanónhsa the home of my spirit.

you are the very kanónhsa the home of my heart.

i have been alive for so many more years than you were in my life. yet no matter how far i moved away in body and spirit you were with me.

and you are with me now.

at my worst moments i can feel your warm calloused hands.

i can hear your warm and kind indian voice.

i can smell your smudging herbs and your medicines.

and that is enough.

you are more than enough.

you are so much more than enough.

my tóta.

you are here with me.

always.

and you tóta are more than enough.

i could legally get away with killing you

i never felt that i had permission to hate my mother.

she was sick with a mental illness. more than one mental illness. more than one illness. her whole family was sick. schizophrenia. paranoid schizophrenia. someone who is mentally ill has no control over their actions. you don't have the right to blame them. you don't have the right to hate someone who is crazy you're not supposed to say that about them that they're crazy but they have psychological problems and their actions are not entirely in their control.

her brother charlie my favourite uncle would eventually stab his wife anne to death and be shot by the police. her sister jackie would kill herself after trying to kill her and my step father and a whole bunch of other people. jackie's oldest son derek pink not my half brother derek a different derek derek pink would beat his best friend to death throw the corpse over the balcony wake up the next morning with the body still on the building's front lawn throw him in the car drive up to sudbury drive back and get arrested for the murder. years later when he got out of prison i asked him why he drove the body back to toronto from sudbury a mining town full of deep holes, and he looked at me in confusion and said well he was starting to stink.

after me she had the last child who survived birth danny and he died in less than a year. she always told me that i killed him. that i knocked his cradle off of a table and i believed her.

i remember being at water street in cornwall where she lived apart from my father and mostly apart from me. i only spent a few weeks here and there to convince the welfare people that i lived with her. she refused to live on the reserve because someone might think she was an indian. she was in fact like most white people of her time a racist who just happened to fall in love with a tall handsome indian. the dark part of course is a given. so her and jack got an apartment right across the river on water street. but trouble started between them more than trouble he started to beat on her and drag her up and down stairs by her hair trying to kill her it seems like the preoccupation my family had with each other was always trying to kill some other family member or of course me. soon after that and jack moved back to the reserve and i went with him. sometimes he would visit my mother and sometimes i would stay with my mother. i remember being in a room on water street and looking up at a cradle. i don't remember what happened next or if anything happened next. but after she killed herself we went through her papers and i found danny's death certificate. aside from being mongoloid that's what they called it then and i remember her screaming for years afterwards that he wasn't mongoloid he was indian that's what they called us then the only time she ever acknowledged that there was anything to do with any of us being indian that's what we were called then. danny died because he had severe internal problems that had left him unable to absorb nutrients. he died of slow very slow starvation.

there was no mention of injuries from a fall.

she was a heavy smoker and was on many prescription pills including thalidomide as far back as when she was pregnant with me. after danny there were other pregnancies but none of them made it to birth the last being so cancerous that they gave her a hysterectomy to stop the growth. i escaped my birth with only asperger's and dyslexia. but in her mind i was somehow responsible for the death of not just danny but for her pregnancy problems that followed. somehow in her mind i had taken the best of her body and left none for any of those that followed.

in her mind i was a curse.

in her mind i was a demon. the spawn of some evil indian spirit that my blood father or my tóta who she thought was a witch had placed upon her. danny was a presence that haunted her and haunted me and haunted all of us. danny was a ghost that we carried with us all of our lives.

danny's loss was the thing that tipped my mother over the edge and she was convinced and she convinced me that danny's death was my fault.

for as long as i remember my mother was told by doctors that she had less than a year to live but she was too mean and too angry and too stubborn to die and in the end it was her that ended her life by taking an overdose of pills though my step father my real father and much of my family clung to the idea that it was an accident and it may well have been an accident or it might have been suicide she was always talking about suicide and life for her life for most of my family has been pain and suffering. when i was very young she was diagnosed with paranoid schizophrenia among other things. she would tell me that she could kill me and get away with it because she was certified insane sometimes even when she wasn't angry she would she would say it and then try to kill me.

i could get away with killing you.

when we moved to toronto and her and my step father who would be my real father took me with them though i didn't want to go because i was listed as a dependant on their community housing information and she got really bad. i would sleep in my closet so that she couldn't find me when she got good and stoned from the pills or drunk and came to look for me with a knife. i had learned to sleep lightly as a child because of my father's rage. that served me well when we moved to toronto.

i looked like jack to her and he had badly abused and tormented her as well as me and when she looked at me she saw him and when she looked at me she saw danny and when she looked at me she saw the failed pregnancies and the hysterectomy.

when she looked at me she saw a curse.

how could i blame her.

how could i hate her.

maybe i was a curse.

maybe i was a demon.

and she was a victim. she was not in control.

i did of course secretly in the darkest part of myself blame her and hate her and i hated myself and i felt terribly guilty for those feelings in a way that i did not for my feelings for jack who i felt free to hate and to blame because he wasn't sick. i took out my guilt and my hate and my rage on others including my brother isaac who was blond and perfect and who she loved and my step father loved in way they did not love me because i was hard to love i did not understand it then but the abuse and the asperger's and their own demons made it so but at the time all that i understood was that my parents did not love me therefore i must not be someone or something that could be loved. i got in many fights. almost always with larger boys and groups because i didn't want to win i wanted to lose i wanted to die. just not by her hand or by jack's hands because that would mean they won and i was too mean and angry to give them that.

my survival was not survival but a refusal to lose to them or to lose to her a refusal to lose to the world a refusal to lose.

i got that stubbornness from my mother. i did not recognize it as strength in me or in her but now i can look back and see that she was always stronger than jack. that part of her rage at the world was that she was always stronger than any of the men in her life and that she had been born into a society that said she should bend her will to these weaker men and that this has been the lot of so many women perhaps the true source despite freud and jung of female madness and angst throughout history.

when she died when she committed suicide perhaps it was an accident. she tried so many times but was she really trying or was it all just something she did to get attention out of habit as part of a kind of ritual that she no longer knew the reason for. that night did she take one too many pills or did she finally have enough. when my sister debby and i went through her things and found letters and documents that told us how miserable and terrible her early life had been what a nightmare her first marriage to jack had been by then both of us knew though we had not spoken about it to each other what kind of monster he was she became even more of a victim than she had been.

she did terrible things to my sister and me. after her sister jackie died my mom and my real father dalton adopted jackie's youngest son isaac. she made his life hell too but we contributed to that my sister debby and i became the lesser monsters in that we were just imitations facsimiles of the real thing so it became next to impossible to place any blame for her treatment of him though in my most secret self of course i did. i thought she was jealous of the bond between isaac and my father my step father dalton. or maybe when she looked at isaac she saw her sister jackie who was her parents' favourite and who tried to kill her many times.

and her brother charlie who like her and her sister and her mother struggled with mental illness and later addiction.

they were poorer than poor and the parents i know so little about the father except that he was convinced that my mother was not his child and so by their standards charlie was spoiled and jackie her sister isaac's blood mother was loved because she was beautiful and blonde she was the golden child and so those ripples very much like each other my mother's life was hell and the mental issues so much of who she became was not her fault and yet and yet she hurt us she hurt me often and she made my life hell those ripples of abuse and suffering so very much like each other undulate outwards and we do not even know who or why they hurled that first stone.

as for me i did not and still do not know how to blame her for what she did to me. my pain my suffering my own nightmare needed someone to blame needed to put a face on my horror and since she had psychological problems and i knew that she had been a victim too it was so much easier to make jack my monster and to place all of the blame on him.

we did share moments together moments when she was lucid and not full of hate when we talked about books and ideas and life. i had gotten my love of reading from somewhere maybe from her and she and i shared other things. she loved to paint and we talked about art and she would lay on her bed and smoke and sometimes we would talk about nothing in particular just talk and in those moments we were alike her and i and she even smiled sometimes and i saw the beautiful woman that she must have once been.

she forgot all that when she took too many pills began to drink or had one of her paranoid episodes that were almost always directed at me because at those times i reminded her of jack i was just like him she would say again and again i shared his mohawk blood his dark looks and i think in those times she saw only that he had been so brutal to her and in her pain in her paranoid tunnel vision i was only his spawn i was her curse and nothing i could do would prevent her rages.

i often stayed away from home finding wilderness even when we moved to toronto but just like when i lived with jack i would come home to find my things destroyed because no one dared stand in her path when she was paranoid they were just glad it was me and not them. and i could not blame them. i would probably do the same given the choice and the opportunity.

jack i could blame but her i could not.

nothing she did seemed like her fault. she was sick. she had lived a horrible life.

she was a victim. not a monster.

not like jack.

if she killed me she wouldn't even go to prison.

no one would blame her.

not even me.

not even me.

i did not have permission to hate her.

and so i hate myself for how i felt about her.

i still mostly hate myself for how i feel about her.

i could kill you and get away with it. she would say to me again and again.

it wouldn't be my fault. my mother would say i'm legally insane.

it wouldn't even be my fault.

fernand

your name was fernand.

i don't know if that's the name you were born with or if that was a name you were given later or maybe a name you chose later.

was there more to you than just that name.

i don't know anything about you.

just that you were my grandfather and you were married to my tóta that my aunts and uncles would walk out of any room you walked into. that you were a catholic fanatic and you were constantly saying my tóta was going to hell and that she was a witch and that i didn't like you very much. that one of my names was supposed to be your name but it was misspelled on my birth certificate and so i do not carry your name. you only spoke french though i always believed it was because you refused to speak any other language rather than because you could not speak any other language. so i barely understood you. i'm sure you spoke to me. you must have spoken to me. but i don't remember your voice and i don't remember your face. just a hazy shadow with no delineation or features. and a smell. i don't remember the smell. just that there was one and that i didn't like it. the smell filled every room that you were in and lingered long after you left. i can't remember what it was. just that when i think of you i think of that smell. i remember that you tried to win me over to your side rather than hers. i was the oldest son of the oldest son. and so there was a war for my soul. and you almost won. i learned the old ways but i also went to church and though i was young i was an altar boy and was in early training to be a priest. then one of the nuns said my tóta was going to hell and i was done with the catholic church.

i was supposed to be given your name and they made it my middle name but somebody somehow got it wrong on the birth certificate and it was spelled fernend and even though that's only one letter different it is still not the same name even on the catholic baptism certificate and i hate that they had me baptized someone got it wrong and it's jules jules fernend etc. and etc. delorme because they actually named me after my uncle jules and also made him my godfather and so his name comes twice at the beginning even though i barely ever met the man it is better than ending up with your name because even as a child i sensed the poison in my family oozed from you and maybe someone spelled it fernend on purpose so that i would not carry your name forward.

i'm very happy that it's not the same name.

i know that it is important to me that i do not carry the heavy yet only guessed at burden of your name. even if it is only a difference of one letter it is not your name and i do not want to bear the poison of your name.

did you take that name that french name maybe both those french names because no one knows what our last name was before both names that i was born with one misspelled or were they given to you the way that they were given to so many indian children by the priests or by the nuns or by the hospitals because they believed in kill the indian save the man that's what they said back then except that in killing the indian they killed more than the indian in him and so many left behind just an empty shell that needed to be filled and they tried to fill it with their beliefs with their christian god but it didn't fit. or maybe it would have if they had not done to you fernand what they did to you. i don't know what they did to you just that they did so many horrible things to so many children so why wouldn't they do it to you. they were sent to internment camps for children and maybe to survive he took their christian names and their religion and maybe they did less to you or maybe they did more or maybe it started before you. i don't know even a little bit of your story because i didn't want to know. though you never did a thing to me i knew i felt you to be a monster a ghost a stealer of spirits and today i think you created the monster that was jack my blood father.

but who created you.

who created fernand.

were you made into a monster.

or were you born that way.

if you were born that way was i born with that monster inside me.

you insisted my tóta be buried in a catholic cemetery in the city of cornwall rather than on the reservation as she would have wanted. your name and birthdate are on the gravestone beside hers but you are not buried there. you are buried somewhere else. at least there is that. i don't know how or why that happened but at least there is that. those are the only things that i know about you. i don't even know your death date. i didn't look. i didn't look at your side of the stone except that quick glance to see there was no death date. and that. that was all i needed to know.

i know almost nothing about you fernand.

you are an evil spirit to me.

a ghost to me.

but is that what you were. were you different when my tóta married you. i know that you met at the residential school but if you were not a different man i don't know why she married you. maybe she still had hope you were going to be a different man or maybe at the time she had no choice maybe it was her that changed and not you. maybe she came out of the residential school thinking you were what she deserved or just that you were familiar and she began to question what they the church had done and what they had taught them and began to remember where she came from and who she came from. where you for whatever reason started and stopped who you were to be set in stone at the school a blank slate a brittle and brutal tabula rasa with no roots and no past and no memories except what they taught you perhaps beat into you or worse or maybe you went into the school broken already looking for someone something to belong to something to grasp someone to be and once found you never let go even when it made you do terrible things made you and everyone around you miserable. it was something the school or maybe something else that made you into someone or even something that was a monster to those that should be loved by you and love you.

did others make you the fernand delorme that i knew. did others make you a monster. or is that how you were born. was there anything left of you after residential school that was not what i knew was not what my blood father and my aunts and uncles knew what my tóta saw that was not a monster that was not the fernand delorme that we all knew. or were you even something else before. were you like that before she knew you. where did fernand the fernand that i knew the fernand that we all knew even start.

were you ever sorry for what you did.

did you ever feel real guilt or did you feel that artificial catholic guilt that guilt of the sin that once confessed is forgiven and forgotten and the deepest truths never told never really confessed not even to the self because that's how monsters can be monsters. but did you ever pause to think what have i done or even what was done to me did you even admit that something was done to you because something terrible must have been done to you perhaps many terrible things. but unlike my tóta you became your abusers and in studying psychology because i thought i wanted to know what was wrong with me and what was wrong with my family and the people i knew i learned that stockholm syndrome almost always involves the denial that those who abused you did anything wrong that they were trying to help you which means you are trying to help those you abuse or that they and you deserve the abuse and so there is nothing to feel guilty about. but is it so absolute. are there cracks are there moments where the truth where guilt slips through and you say oh my god what have i done or like king richard a nightmare that slips through in the night or perhaps in that moment before you died was there that moment where that person you were born to be slips through and you are overwhelmed by guilt by shame or was there just mist just darkness and then more darkness because if what you believed was right that there is a heaven and hell then you are suffering. but i don't think that you were right so if you did not feel guilt if you did not feel shame perhaps there is no justice perhaps there is no balance and there is just whatever we see no more than that nothing in balance.

or perhaps there is absolute evil.

do you even belong in catholic hell.

after all you were an indian. would they even let you in.

if we are going to blame where does it begin. and where does it end. does it begin with you with fernand. or with the residential schools. or with the settlers. with all settlers. were they all evil for coming to this land where there was so much or was it just the leaders. were all the leaders evil. were all the priests for instance. the first jesuits. were they all evil. or was the church. or the government. but those things are made up of people. were all the people evil. where do we start and where do we stop. is it for me with you fernand. not that i forgive you and not that you are blameless but do i start and do i stop with you.

where do i begin.

where did i begin.

jack's people my tóta's people were your people though you denied them. and my ancestors were your ancestors though you denied them. i could sometimes feel them on the land some of them died violently but their spirits their spirits did not suffer because they were proud and they had honour and they belonged to something. not that nothing bad was ever done to any of them even before the settlers came but they knew they knew what they belonged to what and who they were. they had their own world and their own gods and their own beliefs and their own language and they were their own people. i could feel them when i was a boy particularly when i was in the deep woods. and i could feel people from other tribes and it was the same they were still people they still fought and they still feared and they still suffered and did bad and good things but they knew what they belonged to they knew who they belonged to who they belonged with. not free exactly. but what they had was of them.

but our people were called maneaters by other tribes and many tribes did this even some of us did this perhaps to take the power from our enemies but we were a relatively small tribe surrounded by enemies and though we formed an alliance we were still dwarfed so it was not a paradise for us and it was not a paradise for our enemies before the settlers came. though at least we had our own way of life and my mother's people whether they were french or irish as she claimed were settlers so half of me would be to blame if the settlers are to blame and then where do we stop where do we start to blame. that makes a difference. you did not have that. at least not when i knew you.

fernand was not the name your people would have given you. you called it yours you believed it yours but it was probably given to you by people who were not your people or was passed down to you by people who were not your people. you were not fernand. not really. i don't know who you were but you were not fernand. a rose by any other name does not know that it is a rose.

tóta had a french name too. therese. a name given to her or passed on to her. a french name just like mine after one of my uncles but she never used it and she knew who she was and what she belonged to and who she belonged to like the ancestors in the forest she had her language my tóta her ancestors language and her beliefs and her medicine and she taught some of that to me. maybe that's why i survived why my spirit survived through all the horror through all the abuse the not being loved by anyone but her and perhaps that is why i can carry my french names and still be who i am by any other name.

you tried to love me. well. what you would have mistook for love or perhaps called love. but your version of love was bent and warped and tried to make me into someone else something else. tóta and even my blood father and my uncles and aunts made sure i was never left in a room alone with you but i saw in your eyes what you would do and that you would see it as love or something like it and i felt your spirit your unquiet damaged damaging spirit and so i too avoided you but i knew that you wanted to love me but that what you called love would come in the form of a harm that was worse than the terrible harm my blood father did to me and my mother did to me and so many others did to me your harm would warp me forever would kill the little bit of love that i still carried inside of me the little bit of me that i still had inside of me and so i avoided you i developed a repulsive field that kept you at a certain distance unless there was someone in the room and even then i forced myself to let you touch me and when your touch lingered too much i found a reason to move away from you i didn't hate you not exactly not the way i hated my blood father i just was repulsed by you by an instinct by a knowing that went beyond knowing and i know that it hurt you a hurt that became anger that i chose my tóta over you but there was no actual choosing that i remember there was only instinct and knowing beyond knowing.

did he hate you the way that i hated him.

did jack hate you in the way that i hated him.

i think that he did. i think that he hated you even more than i hated him. i would see flashes in his eyes. in all my uncles' and aunts' eyes. they hated you. my tóta too. she hated you for whatever you did to her children. not what you did to her. though i am sure you did things to her at least in the past when you could. i think my blood father and my uncles and other people of the reserve eventually stopped you from abusing her because she was a clan mother and a medicine woman but you did abuse her because abuse was what you did what you called love it was what you were it was all any of us knew about you.

stories travel in a circle.

blame travels in a circle too.

your name was fernand.

there was more to you than that.

there are no answers in your name.

there are no answers about you at all.

fernand.

just a name.

just your name.

what's in a name.

except that i know that i'm glad that i do not carry it.

it may be a small difference but it is enough.

fernend.

not fernand.

not fernand.

there is something in a name.

kaia'tákerahs

i have had many friends in my life who did not walk on two legs.

so many.

you kaia'tákerahs you goat were among the first.

you belonged to my tóta though she did not believe that any living thing could belong to any other living thing. i named you william william goat as in billie goat despite the fact that you were female but i always just called you goat.

when i first met you you were fiercely protective and territorial about my tóta's house especially the front yard. you had a simple rule. anyone who went into that house had to come and greet you to be approved by you before they entered tóta's house. one time a mountie who had come to the reserve to look for one of my uncles walked into tóta's house without being approved by you and started to yell at her. it shocked us all because she was a clan mother and a medicine woman and his behaviour was so disrespectful. he was a big man. a very big man. he filled the entire doorway. and when he stepped through the door to leave you charged and butted him right in the balls. you were so much smaller than him but he went down so hard. an ambulance had to come and carry him away. he tried to have you put down and we had to hide you for a while but the laws did not cover what you a four legged being did to him back then and even his fellow mounties made fun of him for trying to take it to court so he dropped it.

you became a hero on the reserve and because by then you'd taken to following me everywhere and people had already started to call me kaia'tákerahs because of that i became briefly popular too.

i don't remember why you took to following me everywhere on the reserve. i didn't feed you. i didn't have any food even for myself tóta fed me when she could. but my uncles were always there eating her food and though he was not a big man my grandfather ate a lot too. of course she fed you but you goats eat almost anything and you often did.

i played with you and petted you but many people did i think. perhaps because i would put my head up against yours to greet you and you began to think i was another kaia'tákerahs. head butts were part of your language and putting your head against another's was a form of affection. i spoke your language. certainly others on the reserve thought so because they began to call me goat jokingly but kept calling me kaia'tákerahs because when i got angry i would put my head down and charge and keep charging no matter how they beat me. sometimes you joined me and we charged together or took turns charging. i called you kaia'tákerahs and they called me kaia'tákerahs.

we were more than friends. we were siblings.

when my tóta died. you officially became my goat although i still did not think you belonged to anybody and i do not think that you thought of yourself as belonging to anybody. i just went from being your best friend to your only friend. you were my sister. other than when i was in school we were always together.

always.

and then my mother and my step father moved to toronto and they had to take me because they were claiming me as a dependant. i didn't want to go for so many reasons. i didn't want to leave the reservation. i didn't want to live with a family that were basically strangers to me. i didn't want to leave my one true friend roger or my few casual friends to go to the big city where there would be no wilderness and there would be so much concrete and steel.

and i didn't want to leave you kaia'tákerahs.

i could not tell anyone except roger that i did not want to leave you. i made him promise to take care of you and i knew he would but he told me you died shortly after i left and you were very old but i felt and i still feel that it was my fault that you died that you died from a broken heart and i still miss you i can still feel your head against mine i can still smell you i can still feel you nibbling on my ear my right ear which you so loved to do. oh goat. oh kaia'tákerahs. i still miss you. with all of my heart with every ounce of me i do even though most people do not understand missing a kaia'tákerahs so much loving a goat so much. kaia'tákerahs. i do love you even though you have been gone a very long time and no one has called me goat in a very long time. maybe you would have died when you did even if i had of stayed. maybe.

i have had many friends who did not walk on two legs.

more than those who walk on two legs.

better so often than those who walk on two legs.

purer.

truer.

sweeter.

you kaia'tákerahs were the first.

i still miss you.

my friend.

my family.

my sister.

kaia'tákerahs

our heads

our heads will meet again.

maureen

i escaped your madness maureen.

did you know that. did it even occur to you that your children might end up like you and your siblings. that debby and i did not end up with the schizophrenia that plagued you and your sister jackie and your brother charlie. we ended up with other problems which perhaps were inevitable when you account for the different kinds of abuse we both suffered.

isaac my brother was terribly angry for the longest time but that is largely down to debby and i who took our abuse out on him. we tortured him because he was the only person that we could torture. but he is not mentally ill. he's actually doing great now. a happy healthy grandfather. my nephews and my niece may have their own problems because of their own abuse or perhaps the worlds they grew up in but none of them show signs of paranoid schizophrenia. it seems to have stopped with you and your siblings.

would that make you happy.

would you have enjoyed meeting that next generation or now the one after that. i often thought that you were a narcissist but now i think that your illnesses mental and physical made you self absorbed but i think that in your own way you loved your children. would you love their children. would you love their children's' children. or were you in the end so self absorbed so cloaked in your own pain and madness that you would not have even taken notice or may have even been angry that we got off in a way easier than you and your sister and your brother.

on that very last day the day before easter the day before you died i had visited you without knowing why. i cancelled a date with a girl i'd been trying to get together with for years. i never did get a date with her. we sat at the kitchen table while dad dalton my real father lay in his room and read and you and i spoke in an easy comfortable way that we had not done since i was a child and as i was leaving as i was walking out the door i stopped and turned and told you that i loved you.

i don't know why i did that.

i did not even think that i meant it then.

you were so clearly shocked.

we were both so shocked.

we did not say those things in our family.

but we hugged and that night you killed yourself whether by accident or on purpose and debby called me the next day easter sunday you were dead and i was ready.

something or someone had given me a gift.

or perhaps it or they gave you a gift.

you died knowing that at least one of your children loved you.

because i know now that i did mean it that i did love you i do love you because perhaps you didn't even do your best but you meant to do better. i think you started out wanting to give us what you were never given not from your mother and certainly not from your father and not from jack no definitely not him. but i think you did get from dalton though his focus became on protecting us from you and then somewhere along the way he just gave up. your rage and your madness filled all of our worlds but perhaps that night you were not angry. that is not why i did what i did and said what i said though i did not think that i meant it then.

i still don't know why i said i love you.

but if it gave you some peace then at least there is that. it took me years to find feelings in me other than fear and hatred and blame inside me for you. so i do not take credit for what happened because i did not mean to give you peace. i just acted on some instinct some voice that was not my own. i was pushed towards you that day and to say the things that i did and that act gave me peace and it may have given you peace but it did not come from me i did not even know what i was doing or why i was doing it and so i take credit only in obeying the push and i do not know who or what pushed me or if it was for my sake or for your sake or for both our sakes i am thankful to those who taught me to listen to calls like that one and obey them when they have come.

i have come to know that i meant it when i said i loved you. i do love you. i forgive you for much of what you did to me and to debby and isaac though it is up to her and up to him to decide if they forgive you. i felt so much anger so much rage that you did those things not just to me but to us and you almost certainly felt that there was nothing to forgive. some of what you did i still cannot forgive despite what i know about you and perhaps i will never be able to forgive. i try each day to forgive more of what you did as i would like others to forgive me but i do not always succeed.

i have wronged many others.

so much damage has been passed on. what i did to isaac is what you and jack did to me and though i am very sorry that i did these things i do not expect him to fully forgive me in the way that i cannot fully forgive you.

for most others my sin was the sin of neglect which in so many ways is more vile in that so many of those others do not even think that they have been sinned against. i left them behind thinking that there was something wrong with them in that i did not love them the way that they deserved to be loved i made them think that my neglect and my eventual abandonment of them abandoning them as i was so often abandoned as a child was their fault. i was not capable of the kind of love and that included commitment i am still not capable of that kind of love because i did not know that kind of love but i could have tried to do better as i am trying now. i told myself that since i was not guilty of physical or verbal abuse of anyone but isaac that i was somehow better than you or jack but that was and is setting the bar so low that it was very easy to feel i had done enough that i am doing enough.

i do not blame you.

you were sick and knew nothing but abuse and i made and make my own choices. i am the one responsible for the damage that i have done. including to you. maybe i undid some of that damage when i left on that last day because what i did to you as i have always done and am still doing to isaac and so many others was to neglect you and make you feel unloved.

you were not easy to love but i could have done better.

i have made myself not easy to love in the way that i am still capable of neglect and of disappearing from people's lives. i saw and many others saw my lack of attachment was a kind of strength and it was when i was young in that it allowed me to survive more intact the abuse and the neglect and the black hole of identity that i was born and raised into. but what allowed me to survive my youth on the akwesasne reserve made me a weak human being later. as is so often true the survival strategies we develop as children work well to keep us intact then but make us into adults who were constructed by a child. i continued and continue to avoid attachment out of fear and habit rather than courage.

and yes there is the asperger's that's what we called it then but i have it. it does not have me.

i could and would fight anyone run into fires jump out of planes make leaps that others might not make but when it came to being with my fellow human beings i was and am a coward.

that is not your fault.

that is mine.

i escaped your madness.

but i did not escape your fears.

i did not escape your flaws. and in trying to overcome them i think i understand you much more.

i am older than you were when you died. and in my old age with my passions ebbing i am learning how to love. it is not easy. it requires a courage that i do not always have.

and my fear and my distance from others is its own kind of madness.

not as obvious as yours.

not as blameless as yours.

i have escaped your kind of madness.

i still wrestle within to find my own courage every day.

every single day.

sometimes i feel that i am winning. sometimes i feel that i am losing.

there is no escaping me. no escaping the rage and the hate and the fear. perhaps that is the beginnings of sanity.

that knowing.

that knowing that there is no escaping from me.

but i know this. i did and i do love you mother.

i do love you maureen.

my mother.

i escaped your madness.

i did not escape.

nor do i seek to escape.

that i am your son.

spirit walk

i feel the snow crunch beneath my feet.

the ice dangles and glimmers from the branches of the trees.

glistening diamonds everywhere.

it is my spirit walk. me and kaia'tákerahs have just crossed polly's gut on the first day of our spirit walk. well it is my spirit walk i don't know about goat. she will stop to forage and eat and drink and will have no problem catching back up to me. four legs are so much better than two. perhaps for her it is spiritual. i do not believe as some people do that animals are not spiritual. we humans are animals and some of us are spiritual. i think the same applies to them. i've seen goat standing still staring at a tree or a rock or by the creek and maybe she was seeing or hearing something or communing with something that i could not.

it's tsothohrhko:wa january. the big cold. but it's not that cold not warm but not as cold as it usually is this time of year. cold enough so the ice and the snow aren't melting but not so cold that it stings the skin. but that might change so i've put some extra warm clothes in my old backpack just in case.

i'm extra careful crossing polly's gut in case the ice isn't solid. brought my walking stick and carry it cross my body the way i've been taught until i get to the other side. hear a few small cracks but nothing to really worry me. make it across no problem. coming back might be a problem.

it is early in the walk and i feel strong. i never have problems on the walks. i can walk for days without eating or drinking or sleeping and hardly feel it. i could probably run for days if i want to. this is what i was built for. on the second or third day i'll start to see things. that's the point. i already built the sweat lodge in the woods by the creek for the end of the walk. if i don't see things on the walk i'll definitely see them there. i don't tell any of the white people in my life because they wouldn't understand. they'd just think it's crazy.

especially because i might die.

that's part of the point. every single walk i might not make it back. that's part of the deal. being intimate with death makes you more alive makes you aware what a miracle it is to be alive and no matter how we try we don't have any real say in how long we get to stay in this world and when death comes for us.

i am just a child but i see adults most adults who don't seem to understand this who lie to themselves about how tenuous our grip is on this life. if they were to live every day as if they might die tomorrow how much better their lives would be. but instead they lie to themselves and pretend they have some control and pretend they have forever to do the things they want to do.

i am just a child but i know this.

goat rubs up against me as we walk. it is a comforting feeling for me. i don't know if she does this so often because she likes it or if it is just accident. the spirit walk is supposed to be done alone and i have no problem with that but goat will not be left behind for three days and like all kaia'tákerahs and like me she is stubborn.

like me she is stubborn.

besides being alone simply means being without other human beings. human beings talk too much they are too needy even when they are quiet very few human beings know how to be with you without crowding your spiritual space. i know two people who do and that is more than most people will ever know. animals never interfere with spiritual vision. i try my best to return the favour.

i am just a child but i know how to do that.

i am just a child but i know how to do that.

goat has always known how to do that.

we walk. soon there will be woods. i can walk for all three days of a spirit walk in the wilderness if i so choose. but the spirit walk is not about choice. you are led. you do not choose where to go. so far somehow i always end up home but perhaps one day the walk will lead me somewhere that i will not come back from.

my life is not much to lose.

that is how it seems to me at the time.

that is how it often seems to me now.

if this walk does not kill me then my father or my mother might any day. they both have come close before. perhaps a bully or a gang will kill me. that too has come close to happening more than once though i always leave some hurt and damage in my wake. perhaps i will die of starvation or malnutrition or get hit by a car i often wander into the road lost in my own thoughts or i'll freeze to death because we almost never have any electricity or i'll run into a bear or a pack of wolves or some other animal or i'll die from some disease or be killed by one of my seizures or fall into a hole.

so many ways to die.

more ways to die than there are to live.

and for me death is the ending of my suffering but i am too stubborn to actually just give up and die easily. the bear has to win the fight.

even now i have come to love life and those in my life but dying is no big thing for me. it's going to happen. and when it comes i will fight because fighting is what i do but not because i fear or dread death but because death the great bear must use all of her teeth and her claws and her strength if it wants to take me. i will not go gentle into that good night.

we reach the treeline and goat dances among the trees. she is always happy to be in the woods. perhaps because that is where i am the happiest and i often dance with her when we reach the woods. today i am conserving my energy since this is only the beginning of my walk though i do speed up and my step lightens. it is hard not to dance when goat dances. she dances with all her joy.

i wish i could dance with all my joy.

i wish i could do anything with all my joy.

the only thing that i have ever abandoned myself to and the only thing that has ever taken complete hold of me has been and would be rage. no. that is not true. when i am in nature and when i am with my four legged friends i often lose myself and know true and absolute joy. but my family is very good at rage. my family is very good at violence. my life does and will for a long time revolve around violence. in the world that i grew up in capacity for violence earns you respect and i had that capacity in spades.

i am too strange to be popular.

i often cry while beating the crap out of someone far bigger than i am.

other kids want to make fun of me but are often too frightened by my capacity for violence my capacity for rage. but the fact that i can fight should make me cool. it doesn't. i always have snot running down my face i stand sometimes staring at nothing and i wear clothes that even the poorest kids make fun of and i walk around for most of the year in bare feet because when someone does buy me shoes i lose them.

i am not cool at all.

bigger kids and gangs of kids come after me because i am strange and because on the rez i am half white and in the city i am half indian. i usually cause too much bloodshed too much injury usually as much as my own for them to repeat the attacks and yet i am in a fight at least once a week. because of my temper and because i know no other reaction nothing to turn to but violence.

it is all that i know. it is all that i'm good at.

that is how i see myself then. at one point someone asks jack why he hits me and he tells them it's all that i'm good for.

kaia'tákerahs has a temper too but she gives herself over to other things. in that way she is far more spiritually developed than me. in that way she is a teacher to me. she teaches me that joy is a thing too.

and so i walk a little more lightly while goat dances among the trees.

what more can you ask for from a companion.

what more could you ask for from a friend.

we walk.

to we know not where.

or if we will return.

we walk.

our bodies walk.

our spirits walk.

this is what we do.

in some way or another.

this is what we will always do.

even long after she is gone.

there is no spirit walk without goat.

and spirit walk will always be a big part of my life.

and so we walk.

and walk some more.

and walk some more.

the snow crunches beneath my feet.

and i walk.

and we walk.

my friend and i.

kaia'tákerahs and i.

debby

debby.

my sister.

my beautiful sister.

you did not start out life as the person you became.

your children only know you as the person that you became and no matter what i say or do you will be remembered by them and so many others as that person. drugs and alcohol and abuse of every kind turned you into someone else into someone so unlike the sister that i knew growing up that even i thought of you as a drug addict as an abuser as a liar as a thief and all of the so many terrible things that we thought about when we thought about you.

but you were so much more than that.

all that i knew when i was young was that you were never sent with me to live on the reserve with our blood father to avoid the abuse and the rape that was then a part of what was done with all that anger and the generations that learned to hate others and hate themselves and hate the indian that was what we called it then in themselves and in others. i thought that i was sent there alone because no one wanted or loved me and the reserve was just the dumping ground for what no one in our family wanted. i did not see what happened to girls in that place at that time and i did not think that you would almost certainly not have survived jack's abuse though at that time and for so many years to come i thought him incapable of what he would do to you and perhaps to others and i look back at fernand our grandfather and how when he would walk into a room jack or my uncles or aunts would walk out of the room and how i never heard my tóta even speak to him though he spoke often to her mostly to tell her that she was going to hell for practising traditional medicine and that she was a witch and not going with him to church how none of his children not jack or my uncles went to church perhaps because that was his place and what he had learned from residential school. i thought that i was on the reserve because no one wanted me and you my sister got to stay at glenview in the city and later the children that jack had in another city with another woman were also kept away from the reserve hardly even knowing that they were indian that's what they called it then.

and i never told you the truth about jack.

even when we moved to toronto and were thrown together and you and i became so close taking walks and sitting under trees and telling each other secrets but i never told you that the jack that i knew was a monster. though i did not think he was the kind of monster that he turned out to be. you would talk about him a man at that time you had barely met and who seemed so handsome and charming and you would talk about him as the father that you wished you had and i never told you what he did to me. it was the secret. it was my secret. only mine. i kept it from everybody else. but maybe if i had told you if i had said something anything about the monster that lived inside that handsome man you would not have gone to him later and he would not have had a chance to do to you what he did to you the unspeakable thing that he did to you. you were so innocent then so beautiful the most beautiful girl in our neighborhood. maybe i didn't want to spoil your illusion or maybe i had hidden the beatings for so long maybe the last thing that i wanted to admit was that i was a victim.

i don't know.

but we sat under trees and talked mostly you talked and i listened and i never told you i never told you what living with him was like it was my secret and i held on to it greedily like it was something precious or something i had to keep out of the light even from you. yes. greedily. i treasured my abuse and hid it in the dark like some mythical creeping bony thing because that is the only thing that i had that was mine and only mine.

there it is. it makes no sense but there it is.

i'm sorry that i never told you debby.

and you fought with mom you always fought with mom and we both gave dad our real father dalton the man who stayed and raised us and did not abuse us any of us we gave him such a hard time perhaps because we did not know that he was as good as it got for us that we were lucky to have him in our lives to keep mom from killing us in her fits of madness that way her brother and sister did dalton the man who starved himself sometimes to feed us and raised us. maybe he showed isaac more love because isaac was given his name and we kept jack's name though we didn't even know why and we both gave dad our real father the man who stayed such a hard time but i knew deep down how lucky we were that he was in our life and not jack. and maybe he could not bring himself to tell us about what jack had done to our mother he could not bring himself to tell us about many things because he was raised to speak little and to keep secrets and not to show much. we were all raised to keep secrets and to speak little and to say nothing of our family or what our family did just this empty taciturn space that got passed down from generation to generation with secrets getting added to secrets until there were too many and too much silence to be bridged.

but you did not do drugs and you almost never drank and you did not lie at least not to me and you were beautiful and you had dreams and were filled with laughter.

and then you left and moved to kitchener near to where jack was living with his new family and i did not say anything. and then i heard that you were living with jack and his other family and i did not say anything. i just hoped he had changed i did not believe he would ever do to a girl what he had done to me i believed he had done to me what he did because i was me and it was my fault. and mom never told us about the way he had abused her that we later found out in letters after she died and dad our real father the man who raised us never told us that he had rescued her while jack was in prison and moved her from water street to glenview so that when jack got out he only had me and his other family to abuse and we all kept his secret and none of us were keeping his secrets we were keeping our secrets because that is how abusers get away with it people don't keep secrets to protect the abusers but to protect themselves to not be seen as a victim or in dad's case because that's what he was raised to do. so that you did not know who he really was until it was too late and years later you would come home and you were on drugs and you had changed and you never stopped lying or stealing until nothing you said could be believed and one day i was visiting and you were drunk and you said that jack had raped you and let other men rape you and we did not believe you not me or mom or dad we thought he would beat his wife and children but surely he would not do that and we sat there at there at the kitchen table with the yellow nicotine stained ceiling over where mom always sat and smoked and we did not believe you.

we did not believe you.

i did not believe you.

after all that man had done to me i did not believe when you said he had done worse things to you. yes. yes. i was jealous. i was jealous. for so long i had owned my abuse like some precious thing and there you were there you were taking away my right to believe that my abuse was the worst.

we all knew that jack had done and would do terrible things. he had tried to kill me and mom pulled mom down the stairs when she was pregnant with me and stomped on her belly. jumped up and down on her belly. you and i did not know this then. like me mom never spoke about what jack did to her maybe she too did not want to admit she had been a victim of his beating and his shamings and his dragging her by the hair through the street and up the stairs at the water street apartment and beating her so badly that she spent weeks in the hospital and that was just one time she was a proud woman our mom and perhaps she never talked about how horribly she had been abused because that would make her feel like and look like a victim and we would find out only some of it in letters that she never sent to anybody after she had died and we did not know that dad knew what jack had done to her but he sat there and he knew and mom sat there and she knew and i sat there and i knew what he had done to me though i did not know he had started before i was even born i knew but in a different way a way i couldn't even say to myself i knew the violent monster that he could be.

but i did not think he would do that. none of us believed that he would do that. he had been to prison. his friends were all gangsters and bank robbers hard men who hid out with him on the reserve and had respect for him because hard men have a code and jack was a hard man and expected to live up to that code. and the code definitely most definitely did not permit doing that it was one thing to hit a boy especially a child as unlovable as awkward as weird and as stubborn as me but it was quite another to do harm to a girl. surely. even i thought surely jack would never cross that line. these hard men saw him as a stand up guy a guy who went to prison rather than speak names hitting a weird boy which he rarely did in front of them anyway was one thing. jack would never do what his father fernand did.

maybe we wanted to believe that there was good in him some lines he would not cross or else we had been fools for loving him at all and at some point we had all loved him even dad our real dad dalton considered him a good friend once upon a time or maybe we had gotten in the habit of not believing you though you had been the kind of liar you had become for so much less time than you had been that other beautiful girl to me that loving honest sister to me that i knew for so many years. you had only been this manipulative drug user for a few years then. one should have outweighed the other. time should matter. we didn't want to let go of our illusion of jack. i guess it wasn't quite love. but an illusion that despite it all there was some good in this tall handsome man.

whatever the reason each of us sat there and said nothing but convinced ourselves and later convinced each other not to believe you. maybe we each in our own way believed you deep in our hearts. but in our minds we convinced ourselves that it was just another one of your lies.

i am sorry debby for not believing you.

i am sorry sister that i did not believe you.

i was given the grace by your son shawn and your daughter tabitha when you almost died and they found me and called me after i had once again done my disappearing act for years that i got to tell you to your face that i believed you now. i was given the grace when i visited you when shawn told me and told me you were going to die. i rushed up to pembroke and you lived that time and when you got out i told you that i loved you so much.

and i told you that i believed you. i looked into your eyes and i told you that i believed you about jack.

there was a moment. a very long moment. your eyes glazed with tears. and our hearts.

our hearts touched.

for just a moment.

we were brother and sister.

time had passed since i had cut you and everyone else out of my life. i could look at you and see the girl the person that i knew so well as a child when you did your best to protect me and to help me and to befriend me before jack and the drugs and your failures as a mother though what else could you do but fail. that is why i never had children why i chose to play it safe so that i would not become jack or mom but i was strange i was born strange and no one liked me anyway and those that did i felt that i had fooled like groucho said that he would never join any club that would have him as a member and those that liked me those that loved me those that like or love me now are being fooled and i could never love them will never love them because they are foolish or broken enough to love me. the way so many were with jack but you wanted to be loved and you were loved but you could not love yourself and you could not be a parent because nothing you knew was love not true love as a child and so you abused yourself and those you loved and i blamed you for it i did what was easiest for me to walk away and forget instead of staying and trying to help and for that to you and to your children shawn and to tabitha and to tyler i will forever be sorry. i was so angry and damaged that whenever there was the first or the slightest sign of trouble i walked i turned away from everyone but most of all from you and from isaac and your children it was so easy it is so easy to turn away even from life though life would not turn away from me and it was so easy so cowardly and for that debby my sister i am so sorry and i know that i said it to you as i have said it to so many but those are just words and words come easy to me they do not change that i failed you and i failed so many it is not enough but maybe perhaps i can tell the story the truth not just of who i was and am but of who you were before jack broke you all to pieces and even who he might have been before fernand broke him all to pieces and even who fernand may have been before the residential school and the priests and the nuns and even they even they were part of a broken system that was the result of men trying to make the world what they thought it should be with no love for what it was and then tried to make people into what they thought they should be with no love for what they were and it goes on blaming and fixing and fixing and blaming with no love no actual desire to love what is rather than what you think it should be. and i stopped loving you and resented you for what i thought you should be and what you shouldn't be and all you really needed to be was my sister was debby and that should have been enough but instead i grew angry and i turned away i walked away because you were not enough and the world was not what i thought it should be.

i am not a child i am not a young man and i know i know that i should love the world as it is as i would have it love me as i am but every day every single day i wake up and i am angry and i am hurt that the world is not what i want it to be and i blame the system i blame them there is always a them or a they.

you started out so honest and with such huge caring heart.

and you are gone now.

and i am old now.

but sometimes in fact often i think of you debby.

my beautiful sister.

of your children.

of isaac.

and his children.

and know that i have not been what brothers are supposed to be.

but through it all though i did not get it right.

i did love you.

i do love you.

not the way i was supposed to love or the way that i should have loved.

but you were my sister debby and i never stopped loving you.

and i'll never stop loving you though you are gone.

and my chance to get it right is gone too.

you are still my sister.

and you always will be that.

you did not end up who you started out to be.

but to me you will always be.

debby.

that beautiful and kind girl.

my sister.

debby.

i am your brother.

you are my sister.

my beautiful sister.

forever.

asperger's

asperger's.

sounds like ass burgers.

that's what they called it then.

well. not exactly. in the beginning the diagnosis was unheard of and they said i might be somewhere on the spectrum exactly what they would say today. but i had the unfortunate fortune of having a therapist who had actually studied in switzerland and so the word was used even before it became accepted as an official diagnosis.

when my brother first heard that word he made fun of me non stop. i was among the first in canada to be diagnosed with asperger's.

ass burger's.

but first they had said i was somewhere on the spectrum. high functioning autism.

high functioning.

i had worked so hard with my older friend roger and with my tóta on the reserve to appear more functional more normal. things like meeting people's eyes and speaking even when i didn't want to. not habitual rocking in public and avoiding human touch refusing to shake hands. all of those things that made me unable to communicate with other people. i worked so hard. they worked so hard. it was exhausting to learn to do things that were completely against my nature and it was exhausting for them to teach me.

so when they said high functioning i wanted to tell them that i was barely functioning. that it was all i could do to do the things they saw me do.

and then they told me i had asperger's syndrome.

and all my friends all the people that cared about me and even the people who didn't eventually asked me in some way what it was like and i tried to tell them i really really tried but i don't know anything else i don't know any other way of being i don't know what it is like inside someone who is normal so how do you explain when you don't know what the colour red is to a blind person. people tend to assume that autistic people feel less or sense less but the truth is that i feel so much i sense so much that i am overwhelmed and i sometimes need to shut down to the outside world to create filters to make it all bearable. at least that's how it feels to me.

but that only begins to describe what it's like.

there is nothing i wanted more growing up than to be normal to just fit in. i would have done anything not to draw attention to myself but everything i did everything i said seemed to make others make fun of me and pick on me or just stare at me in lack of understanding.

i am an old man now. i can look back and see that not being normal was a kind of advantage. i could see things that other people couldn't see. i could see the world in a way that others could not see. that was what my tóta saw in me. that was what made her single me out.

when i was young asperger's seemed like a disease.

now that i'm old looking back i see it not as a disease not as a disorder but as a gift.

that was how my tóta saw it.

that is how most indigenous people see being different.

it is not all that i am.

but it is a big part of who i am.

it may be a funny sounding word.

asperger's.

ass burgers.

it may make some people laugh.

i may make some people laugh.

that's okay.

now i would have it no other way but to be me.

i'd rather be me than everybody else.

roger

i have been blessed with many true and magnificent friends throughout my life. i have even had many wonderful two legged friends.

life did not bless me with much but with that i have been a truly wealthy human being.

i have known many people many people who did not even have one friend that they could trust absolutely that they could turn to no matter what the problem was as they could turn to me even when we went years without seeing each other.

you roger were and are the very best among those glorious friends.

you did not start out to be my friend.

people on the reserve called you billy as in billy jack from the movies. at that time only the *born losers* the first film in the *billy jack* series was out but you dressed and you acted like him. you fought like him. and we did not know that the actor was white and we watched *born losers* again and again because it was an indian that's what we called it then beating up on white people and the roxy theatre across the river that my step father dalton had worked on building was crowded with indians and we cheered and shouted at the screen because that was the first time any of us had seen a modern indian as the hero of a movie and it would only be later long after the *billy jack* movies that we would find out that tom laughton the actor was white and even then it didn't matter because it was a movie about a modern indian beating up white people.

and you loved horses and you dressed like him and you even spoke like him and you had studied hapkido which was what the martial art that *billy jack* used and you decided to teach me because even though i already knew how to fight one of the few things that everybody in my family even the women were very good at was fighting i was always in fights with bigger kids or outnumbered back then being a half breed was not normal there were many more fbi's full blooded indians that's what we called them then than there are now and so i got picked on by people on the reserve for being half white and i got picked on in the city for being half indian by bigger kids and gangs of kids and you decided to teach me not because you liked me or felt sorry for me i think maybe you did but mainly because my tóta my grandmother was a clan mother of your clan and my clan and a medicine woman and you were older than me and i was awkward and snot nosed and angry and not easy to like but you revered my tóta. first you began to teach me hapkido and then how to hunt and be in the woods and how to ride though my blood father was a very good horseman too he would never teach me and i looked up to you and i wanted to be you and every time i was sent to the city i wanted to run back to the reserve to be with you and my tóta even though in the city i was fed and clothed and much better taken care of you were not there and my tóta was not there and so i always wanted to go back to the reserve even when jack was gone or when he was there and trying to beat me to death all that mattered was you and my tóta even now when people call me white i know that i am not because you and she were and are you and my tóta were and are more a part of who i am than anyone or anything else and even if you did not intend to be my friend you became the very definition of friend to me and i carry you with me as i carry her with me and you are more a part of me than anyone or anything else.

you took me to the ymca and you signed me up for boxing
and wrestling and judo and long before there was such a
thing as mixed martial arts you made me into a mixed martial
artist. at first i was learning to fight in order to survive being
outnumbered or up against much larger and older kids. but
later it became a way of channeling my rage and of not hurting other people of defending the weak and of not drinking
or smoking or doing drugs like every other member of my
family except my uncle jules who i hardly knew and my tóta.
and then my tóta died and there was only you. and then i was
taken to toronto and there was not even you and i began to
devour myself until i found that if i walked and found some
woods as you had taught me that i could survive. even if it
wasn't the same it was just enough for me to not kill myself
or someone else and when i was in the woods or when i was
walking it was like you were with me and i got back to martial arts and boxing and wrestling and it was not the same
without you but it was just enough and then a teacher got
me a forged id because i wasn't actually old enough and i
joined the army. even though i only learned how to jump out
of planes and shoot people while most other people learned
a trade of some kind they put me through school and paid
for my first few years of university. and then somehow you
found me again and we became friends you did not seem so
much older than me anymore and though we both wandered
and drifted apart again and again you were always my best
friend and so much more than that and i stayed with you for
a while when you moved to a reservation on salt river and i
learned to love the desert and the ways of the navajo and the
apache i encountered there and then i drifted away again but
we would see each other now and again and it was like no
time had passed between us and you would remind me again
and again who i was without words and without saying just
by being. and though i often floundered and drifted towards
dark things i never became fully lost because i had you and i

had my tóta inside me and with me. and when i had gone too far like after the car accident when my legs were shattered and i had lost all my money on hospital bills and the doctors said i would never walk again you came and laura came and you kept me from killing myself again and again and the two of you made me exercise and try and then i was walking and the doctors said i would never walk without a cane and not only did i walk i ran and i did martial arts and i got back to training people and soon i forgot that i did those things because you and i drifted and laura died and i forgot who i was what and who had made me who and what i was.

and then one day i got a call from your girlfriend she said that you had been gone for days and asked if had i seen or heard from you. i told her to go check the barn for the horses because i knew that you would set them free if you had gone to do what i thought you had. you were still living in arizona where there were still wild horses. she called me back and said they were all gone. i told her you were dead. you and i had talked many times about what either one of us would do if we found out we had a wasting or debilitating disease. many people that grew up on akwesasne with us died of cancer because of all the chemicals dumped in the water and so we talked about what we would do if that happened to us. we would go to the wilderness and find a bear. preferably a grizzly bear. you were one of the most skilled trackers i knew. you would find that bear and you would fight that bear with your bare hands because the bear had to earn its meal.

there was no note.

there didn't have to be a note.

a few days later i heard back from her that you had been diagnosed with stomach cancer. the chemicals in the water. the fish. i hated fish so i lived longer but i still had to have two operations to have obstructions removed from my intestines.

a month later your truck was found in the rocky mountains in washington state where we used to hike and climb.

you found your bear.

though i mourned your loss i was glad that you died the way that you always wanted to die. i knew that bear had earned its meal.

i often feel you with me especially on my spirit walks which you taught me how to do my very first true walks were with you and you taught me how to build and operate a sweat for the end of the walk. you taught me how to channel and learn from my visions. you and my tóta are always with me on my walks.

you and my tóta are always with me.

i have been blessed with many so many great and true friends.

you roger are the best of those.

you did not start out to be my friend.

and you became you still are something more than just a friend.

there is not a word for what you were or are to me.

friend.

teacher.

guide.

protector.

brother.

you were and are all of those things and so much more.

and so much more.

then.

and now.

you were.

and are.

so much to me.

so much more to me.

than i can say.

trooper

you weren't my very first friend.

you were my first real heart break.

heart break seems like such a small term for how i felt when i lost you.

how i loved you though.

i can still smell you and smell your soft fur. feel you licking my face.

your stinky breath.

you were half wolf and half german shepherd. jack took you because the people who had you could not tame you. could not deal with you. he had a way with animals. jack. he may have been a monster with human beings. well with me and my mother and later on my sister. but with animals he seemed to have an innate genius for communication. whether it be dogs or horses or coyotes or crows he could find a way to get through to them and get them to cooperate with him even when they refused to cooperate with other human beings.

there was an old one eyed wolf on the reserve that was breaking into people's smoke houses and sheds. many people still had smoke houses back then. and this old wolf was so clever that he always figured a way into the smoke house no matter what people did. there was no talk of killing him because there was so much respect for his cleverness and his boldness. but people were getting pretty upset. one day i came home from school and my blood father jack drunk as always and high on whatever as always was sitting on the edge of the woods. at first i thought he was talking to himself. but then i saw the wolf. i wasn't close enough to understand what he was saying but from then on once a week people put a side of meat in that place by the woods and the raids on the smoke houses stopped. i don't know if jack did that. the meat was his idea but it really seemed like he was talking to the wolf and the old one eyed wolf was listening.

but you trooper were the one animal that chose me over him.

we always had a bunch of dogs in the yard and we had to keep you chained up to keep you from killing them. and many of them were pitbulls or rottweilers. but you would have torn them to pieces. and i don't remember when it started but whenever he beat me up too bad i would go to you and you would protect me from him. you would kill him if he came anywhere near us. i would curl up next to you and go to sleep with you licking my wounds and your soft fur keeping me warm for the night.

it got so i was the only one that could feed you or play with you or take you for a walk. you loved the woods. you wouldn't come when i called but if i got into any kind of trouble you came. otherwise i waited patiently by the big rock by the creek and eventually you would come and we would go home together or we would play a while and then go home.

how i loved you.

how i adored you.

one morning as i did almost every morning i went out to hug and pet you before i went to school and something felt wrong. i often get these feelings and they usually mean something though i usually don't know exactly what but something told me not to leave you that day.

i did anyway.

i left you anyway.

i crossed the river and went to school.

i had been taught by my tóta and roger to always listen to those feelings.

i didn't listen to them that day.

and when i got home that afternoon my uncle weepy was there and he told me that you had broken your chain and run out into the road and gotten run over by a truck. this was the third chain you had broken. you always broke them when i was gone and you got it into your head to come look for me. uncle weepy he wasn't really my uncle just a neighbour who sometimes checked on the house when jack was in prison or went on a bender somewhere. we'd find out later that jack had a whole other family that he wasn't telling anyone about. jack wasn't there that day but i don't remember if he was gone for a long time or just that day.

it doesn't matter.

you protected me and i didn't protect you.

we tell stories by repeating things. that's how we tell stories.

maybe it's in the hope that if we repeat them enough they will make sense to us maybe they are like totems that we bring out again and again or maybe by repeating them we hope they will lose their ability to hurt us because we have made them common and we think that if we say things often enough they will lose their meaning.

they don't. they grow larger and heavier and yet we still repeat again and again and then again.

i took you into the woods your body cold and stiff and i buried you and i prayed to your spirit and the spirit of all wolves and all dogs to forgive me for failing you. i know you did and they did because that's what dogs and wolves do they forgive all trespasses that's why they are human being's best friends but i couldn't forgive myself i still can't forgive myself you deserved better from me you deserved the best of me and i can't change the past but i failed you i didn't listen to that voice i should have stayed home with you that day you deserved at least that.

i have learned to listen to that voice when it speaks to me when it warns me and it has saved me heartache and it has saved others heartaches even if i could not save their bodies.

i stayed in the woods for days and wept.

i did not eat and i did not drink and i hardly slept.

those few who knew and those few who i told tried to tell me that i was just a child and that i could not blame myself but i knew they were wrong.

only roger and my tóta did not try to talk me out of my guilt. they knew about my voice and they knew i could have saved you. they knew that guilt while painful to carry and scarring on the soul is not necessarily a bad thing. it can be a powerful if cruel teacher.

how i did love you though.

i can still feel your soft fur and smell your smell.

your terrible stinky breath.

i still love you so.

i still feel you with me everywhere i go.

you weren't my very first love.

you were my first great heartbreak.

i wish there was a mohawk word for the devastation that i felt.

it always feels more true when i say it in kanien'keha.

it still hurts so much.

but that is part of how much i loved you.

that is part of how much i love you.

trooper.

i'm so sorry i didn't save you.

the way that you saved me.

because you did.

you saved me.

you saved me.

not just my body.

but me.

you saved me.

thank you is not enough for that.

niawen'kó:wa is not enough.

trooper.

my friend.

my love.

my love.

i'm sorry.

i am still so sorry.

warriors

i have known many warriors in my long life.

i thought and i made many others believe that i was a warrior.

i fought constantly. i trained in many martial arts and boxing and wrestling. i joined the army and while others learned a trade i learned how to jump out of planes and shoot people. i became a bouncer in some of the roughest bars and was stabbed and shot at. unlike many others who did what i did i wasn't trying to prove anything i was just gravitating towards what i was very good at. at violence.

and i was trying to die.

i didn't have cancer or a good enough reason to go find a bear so i tried to find more and more ways to get killed. i never expected to live long and i didn't want to live long i still don't want to live long i was predicted by so many to die young that i just believe that to be true and when it wasn't i became i become more and more disappointed. i did not want to live a long life. i did not expect to live a long life. every day of my childhood and most days of my youth i came close to death but it would not take me and i was too stubborn to surrender which is how i've always seen suicide a kind of surrendering. i never quit a fight. i do not surrender. i've never even taken a knee in a fight.

i did not fear death.

i feared life.

i fear life.

i was terrified i am terrified by a long life. what others saw as courage what i saw as courage was not courage at all but a kind of cowardice. i sought out death so that i would not have to live life. i feared i would be overtaken by my mother's madness my family's addictions jack's cruelty all the weaknesses that i was surrounded by and that i knew lived inside of me. i was terrified that if i lived long enough i would be revealed to others and to myself as the weakling and coward that i knew that i was.

but death did not take me it did not want me and now i am old and i know that i have not lived the life of a warrior but of a coward.

i have known warriors.

i have seen warriors.

i have studied warriors.

i have been surrounded by warriors and now i see that most of them were women not men and that they were the ones who chose to live while i and those like me sought death and brought death or violence who broke things and destroyed things while the true warriors were building and struggling not for themselves but for those to come. i used to joke that while i could win a fight with almost anybody my mother and my sister who barely came up to my shoulders could still take me. my tóta my grandmother my blood father's mother was the strongest and bravest human being that i knew and i never saw her commit a single act of violence which in my family is an extraordinary thing. laura who died in a car accident the day i decided that i was going to propose to her kept me from killing myself after the car accident that shattered my legs and i was not strong enough to even live but her and roger were strong for me she was strong for me even when i betrayed her and took her for granted again and again she stayed and i thought that made her weak but now i see how strong she was how much stronger than me and so many women have come into my life and held me when i would not stand and i thought they were fools for caring about me someone like me. but it is not weakness to care it is strength.

i am still surrounded by women who care when i do not have the courage to care. jennifer and alana and crin and doctor norma dunning who keeps telling me not to call her doctor but she is among the real warriors of our people and of her people the voice of not just inuit but of indigenous women of which there are far far too few still who study and teach and speak out in the courts and in the assemblies and it has always been the women who tell the stories whether it be by the fires or in the kitchens or with children sitting on their laps women have always been braver than men and stronger than men i do not say this to win favour because in my sixty plus years i have seen that it is true they are the true warriors the true champions of their people and of people in general there are men now there too and two spirit and three spirit and those who have not chosen their spirit yet but they are so much braver than those of us who just played a role and made noise but really did nothing the women and the young and the many spirited they are the warriors not people like me who sought death because we feared life i see it in my niece tabitha who just very quietly does what none of the men in her family have the courage to do and it is the very embodiment of courage they look to me as some kind of hero but they should look to her because the feminine the spirit that choses to live is where the warriors have always been even if they have not been called that the feminine and the many spirited are the strong not those of us who give in to the primitive violence which is so easy which requires no strength or courage which only requires fear and weakness the true warriors have always chosen to live and to build and to endure that is what requires strength and courage. i am now over sixty years old. i do not say this to attract to ally myself with women but because it's true. there are women who are not better than men and there are men who are worthy of being called warriors but in my life i have known very few and i have certainly not been one of those.

i am in blood. stepped in so far that should i wade no more returning were as tedious as go o'er.

oh i have lived a violent life.

the only thing that i can say in my favour is that i was not violent towards those who would not participate or stood less chance than i and that i have not committed as great acts of violence as others in my family. but that is not to say i have not harmed others. i have harmed many others.

my brother isaac in particular. i took all my rage out on him when we moved to toronto and i was alone my tóta dead and roger far away but that was no excuse. and i lied and i hurt someone innocent i hurt isaac my brother i wanted to make him as ugly and as angry and as afraid as me he did nothing to me not then though later what i deserved but not then i hurt him and then i hurt him some more and now people ask why is your brother so angry it is because he was so beautiful and happy and i did not know how to be happy so i made him not happy and then i went away.

and people said i did not drink or do drugs and that was no small or easy thing when i was surrounded by alcohol and drugs in my family and community yes truly that did take some strength but not as much as you might think. when you are as wildly unpopular as i was saying no is no big thing in fact it is rarely offered and i had a good early beginning thanks to roger with martial arts a reason not to drink or pollute my body. i went to university which too was no small thing in my family and i read books and i had been in the army and i was a martial arts master so i was better i was good i was strong i was wise i was someone to look up to.

i seemed to be a warrior in the old ways that people once were warriors.

but i was a coward.

i broke things.

i broke people.

i wanted to die.

that is not the same as not being afraid to die.

warriors fight to live and they fight to help others live.

i have known many warriors in my long life.

i am not one of them.

i spent most of my life not knowing what a warrior looked like.

i thought they were covered in blood and death.

i now look back and look around and know that while many of them are covered in blood and death they do not look like what i was taught what i taught myself to call warrior.

i have known many warriors in my long life.

i did not recognize them for what they were.

but now now i am learning from them.

i now bow my head in honour of their courage then and now and in the future.

i bow my head and i thank them.

i see them and i thank them.

i see them now.

i learn from them now. for the heroes that they are.

for the warriors that they are.

i see them.

i am in awe of them.

and i thank them.

laura

you deserved so much better than me.

all of the women who came in and out of my life convinced that they must have done something wrong because i was so nice and so gentle and had started off so attentive. they deserved more and better than me and i hope i sincerely hope that some of them got better.

but you laura deserved far better than me.

you were so strong and so beautiful and so intelligent and so very good you deserved so much better and so much more than me and i know you were not perfect but i needed to break everything like an angry child because i was a broken angry child but i disguised myself the way that jack disguised himself and i told myself that i never hit a woman or a child or said a bad word to any woman i was with but what i did was as bad maybe worse i made them i made you fall in love with me and then i ignored you i neglected you and i let you think that it must be something that you did something that was wrong with you when all that was wrong was that i was too afraid i was too much of a coward to stay. but you would not let me leave.

you were among the most strong willed and stubborn people i ever met even more stubborn even than me and though i tried to leave you many times you would not let me go and i was unfaithful and neglectful. at one point i left you at lax so that i could have sex with a pair of twins and that was enough you went away and i barely thought about you not because i didn't care but because asperger's has given me the gift of never looking back of walking away from people and never thinking about them no matter how much they matter to me. i was so busy being a rock star and a fighter and a trainer. doing so many things i always did so many things staying busy outrunning the black dog of depression and then in texas i got in a car accident one of so many but this time i flew through the windshield and into a brick wall and i remember lying on the ground covered in something wet my blood and a man's voice with a thick texas drawl saying he's dead. i'm telling you. he's dead. and thinking maybe i was dead and then waking up in a hospital in so much pain so much pain and the doctors telling me i'd never walk again and i had no insurance and all my so called friends disappeared all my money disappeared and you and roger coming and getting me and moving me back to toronto where i could go to hospitals for free in canada and you and roger moving in with me in a basement apartment with me trying to kill myself again and again. i gave up i finally surrendered and defied my own beliefs and all that i had fought for the rest of my life because if i couldn't walk if i couldn't stand up then who was i because everything i knew about myself was physical and you and roger making me do exercises though they were so painful so fucking painful and there didn't seem to be a point and the doctors would keep saying that i'd never walk again and there i was pissing and shitting myself and you or roger cleaning me and me not knowing why either of you are doing it i had been so horrible to both of you swearing at you calling you names and saying things to you that i would never say or thought i would never say to anyone and i did not mean but that were oh so cruel because before the accident i thought my life was taking off i had forgotten and ignored everything that mattered i had turned my back on everything that mattered including both of you especially both of you and why didn't you go away and let me die all i wanted to do was to die there was nothing about me that didn't want to die but after what seemed like a very long while i stood on my own for just a few seconds and then a few more.

i still wanted to die.

just standing for a few seconds wasn't enough and then i took a few steps with a cane and then a few more and the doctors said i would never walk without a cane and i believed them because they were doctors and i tried to kill myself again and again and you or roger always caught me always stopped me. this was the one thing that had brought me to my knees and the one thing that had me ready to surrender life without my legs but then i was walking entire blocks with a cane only because you and roger made me and doing exercises and then i was running and training though the doctors had said it was impossible and people were telling me how strong i was but i wasn't strong you and roger had been strong for me.

and i still don't know why but i saw you as if for the first time and i knew there was no one like you and that my love for you was not just because i owed you so much because i owed you everything but because i had always loved you from the first moment that i saw you and we were so happy for a few months we were really happy i was not even tempted to be unfaithful i don't know how i deserved you or why you stayed but you did and then on the very weekend that i was going to propose you were coming back from your family in brooklyn and i dreamed you were being mauled by a bulldog and your car got crushed by a mack truck.

it wasn't a dream. i woke up the next day with the dream so vivid in my mind and the phone rang and they told me that it happened that your car was trapped underneath a mack truck and the symbol of a mack truck is a bulldog.

they said you were alive inside that wreck for close to an hour.

an hour.

why did i survive so many car wrecks and you died so horribly in this one. why wasn't it me and not you. if the accident hadn't happened we probably would have gotten married and sooner or later i would have been unfaithful because i am jack delorme's son and i did not deserve you. the me that i was then would surely have betrayed you but the old man that i am now that has learned what it means to be betrayed he would deserve you. i wish i could meet you now. you would have been a magnificent old woman. somehow i feel like the cloud of darkness that has always surrounded me found you my dark cloud did that to you though that makes no sense even though my brain does not believe it my heart believes it that somehow i made it happen to you somehow and and i cannot make myself believe that i did not.

you deserved so much better than me.

you deserved so much better than what you got.

you deserved never to have met me.

i didn't deserve you.

but for some reason you came into my life and you made me a better man.

it took time.

it took too much time.

i'm still not the man that deserved you.

but i'm trying.

i'm really trying.

you deserved so much better than me. you deserved so much better than me. maybe when i die i'll be closer to the man that you deserved.

maybe.

probably not.

almost certainly not.

you would have continued growing and you were already too good for most men.

but i am a better man for having had you in my life.

if you were here and maybe you are here maybe your spirit is still here with me that would be enough for you but it's not enough.

it's not enough.

you deserved better.

i'm sorry.

i know that's not enough i know that's not nearly enough but i am truly sorry.

i'm sorry laura.

you loved me better than i loved you.

i know you would say it was not a contest but for me life is a contest and as always when it comes to love i lost.

you deserved better than that.

there are no words for what you deserved just that you deserved better than me.

i wish i could go back and have you never meet me.

maybe without me you could have been happy.

maybe without me you could have gotten all that you deserved.

but i can't do that.

no matter how i wish it i can't do that.

you got me.

like so many others who deserved more you got me and i am
sorry.

i am truly sorry.

and i did

i do love you

that is not enough.

that is not nearly enough.

no.

not for you.

not for you laura.

it's not enough.

it's not nearly enough.

jack

your real name was jacques.

you went by many names.

as long as i knew you you were on the run from the law on the run from something or someone so you changed your name and you hid out.

on the reserve and other men hid out with you and you changed your name like nikakwaho'tà:'a coyote or tsó:ka'we crow or tehahonhtané:ken rabbit except i liked them and i hated you.

and i knew you wanted me to call you dad but i would call you uncle or mister or anything but dad and it embarrassed you especially in front of other people and maybe that's why i did it but i also did it because i did not consider you my father. a father does not do that to a son or maybe he does maybe that's why the world is so screwed up because so many fathers do that to so many sons but that still would not make me call you dad. no matter how much you hit me would not make me call you dad i still will not call you dad not that. anything but that.

of course it made you hit me more. but everything made you hit me more.

when you disappeared i thought you were in jail or on the run somewhere else but you had another family. maybe my mother knew and maybe the other family knew but i didn't know you had other children maybe. everyone knew except me and i was just glad you were gone even if i was left again to survive all on my own it was better than constantly not knowing whether tonight was going to be the night you were going to finally finish it i wanted you to finish it but i also didn't want you to win so like all things in life i was filled with that contradiction and the pain and the shame and the scars and the bruises that i tried to hide and i stayed away from school until they weren't so bad. in those days no one thought to report me it was an indian thing we all showed up like that from fights and beatings and teachers just looked the other way and other kids made fun of us the three indian kids that went to the city school that's what they called us then indians but when i missed too much school they'd call my tóta and she would say it was an indian thing and that was enough and then i'd show up and i was smart so i would get good grades even missing school and they would pretend not to see and i would pretend they didn't see and the next time i hoped you would finish that you would kill me because for me life was just suffering and you were the wellspring of my suffering and so i hated you and i wanted it to end but i didn't want to go down for the count for the final count not to you no not to you and so even my mind violently clashed with itself.

we agreed on this much. you hated me and i hated you and you wanted to kill me and i wanted to die except you could never bring yourself to just finish the thing you never had the courage to be a true killer and i hated you more for that and for so much more than just that.

but now i'm old and i think no i believe that you were not the original source that even your father was not the source because i know that he and my tóta met in residential school and maybe he became a raving catholic and you became an atheist and my tóta returned to the old ways and the old beliefs were all because of that catholic residential school and the priests and the nuns got a taste of how they treat indians that's what they called us that's what they called it when they were being nice. i have the scars on the outside and the inside and you probably had bigger scars and they probably had even bigger and deeper scars and it didn't even start with them we were all taught to hate ourselves and each other what they did to us oh what they did to us our ancestors were mohawk they were kanien'kehá:ka they were never even defeated and never surrendered but they were still treated we were still treated like we had lost a war we had never even fought. where is their confession and their attrition that they made so many of us do over and over again making us think everything we did and everything we thought everything we were and that had nothing to do with being catholic though that doesn't let the church off the hook there was the government and the other churches. it had to do with being white with being european with being a settler and seeing yourselves as the owners of this land as the privileged and the chosen and what that allows you to do to those that you do not consider chosen as equals we got the pope to apologize but what about all the other institutions what about the queen and then the king what about the british government apologizing and making restitution for what they did in canada mostly to people they did not even conquer who even helped them to save this country start there and then find the individuals including our own people who took advantage of us and even though i blamed you i blame you i cannot forgive you maybe i'll never be able to forgive you i do know i believe that you were not the cause but the result and what you did to me was done to you perhaps worse was done to you i look back and i think much worse done to you but my hatred for you has existed for so long i have been clinging to it for so long.

i have to have someone to blame.

i do not know how to forgive you i do not know how to let the hate go even though i know now that you were a man not a devil that you were made by others i do not know where that begins or stops and so i stop with you even though i know that is not fair or reasonable my mind my heart my soul can do no other not yet perhaps not ever.

there is so much hurt.

there is so much anger.

there are so many scars.

i blame you because you are the easiest to blame and not blaming you would let you off the hook for what you did to me and to my sister and maybe to your other children though i don't know that i even heard you tried to make up for what you did and change when you got older. still for me you are the face of my pain you are the face of my rage my rage has a name and it is jack or jacques or john or whatever you called yourself. my mother was sick and what she did was part of her sickness but you could have chosen not to do to me and others what you did or at least i am not ready to admit that you had no more choice than she did.

i have learned to love my mother.

but i do not have even an ounce of love for you.

another man was my father. another man did his best to love me.

though i was very hard to love or to understand by then.

dalton is my father's name.

you are the name of my hurt.

you are the name of my anger.

you are the name of my hatred.

jack.

jacques.

it means the same thing to me.

by any other name.

by any other name.

you will always be

jack.

the black dog is on me again.

theodore roosevelt called his depression a black dog said he had to always keep moving to stay ahead of it. i've spent most of my life on the move trying to stay ahead of the black dog depression.

but what do you do when you can't move and can't stay ahead of the black dog. i'm paying for living a full contact life all the pain and the loss of mobility. i used to love walking i used to love running. now some days i can barely manage to stand. i've gotten old. much older than my years. i've lived a rough life. years of abuse car accidents motorcycle accidents. roger once joked that my ancestors must have made fun of the people who invented the wheel because everyone in my family has wrecked everything on wheels from cars to tricycles. i was a fighter i joined the army and jumped out of planes and hiked with heavy packs got thrown from i don't know how many horses and got in so many street fights that i can't even count. and some days i feel all of that.

i got up and exercised today even though i was in pain and i didn't want to do anything i didn't want to even breathe and i know i'm supposed to feel better because i did something. but i don't. the great black dog is on me he has sunk his teeth deep into the throat of my spirit and won't let me go. and no amount of exercise or cheering up from my friends or medication will make him go away today.

he was on me yesterday as well.

he'll probably be on me tomorrow.

sometimes he stays on me for days.

sometimes he stays on me for weeks.

i don't want to talk about it with friends i hate talking about my feelings in general but this above all because i see in their eyes that they want to help and some of them try to help by trying to talk me out of my depression. but the black dog isn't something that can be talked away or understood by someone who does not know him. even professionals can only act like they understand. they have studied him but that is not the same as knowing him. and medication only helps sometimes. they try switching and then switching again to stay ahead of the black dog. but sometimes there is no staying ahead. especially now that i am old and cannot out walk or outrun him because of the pain and because i fall down. so all there is to do is live with him on top of me and no amount of light can breach the darkness inside me.

when i was younger it came out as anger.

when i was younger it came out as rage.

i did not think of it as depression. my problem was that i was going to hurt someone. that i did hurt lots of someones. and eventually i was going to kill someone. like my uncle or my cousin and so many others who put people in hospitals and those i don't even know about everyone who knew me said i was going to kill somebody it was just a question of when. i thought i was doing better than my mother and jack because i never hurt women or children. i never even said a bad word to them. i always picked a fight with someone big enough and strong enough or groups of people. mostly i won because i learned every type of hand to hand technique and i could endure more pain than anyone i knew. i thought the martial arts would teach me to control the rage to control the fire and it did.

i didn't kill anybody.

and i hurt fewer and fewer people. but i thought i was learning to control the fire and maybe i was because all that was left all that is left is darkness. yesterday i spent the morning crying for no reason at all. today i am angry. today i am bitter.

i don't want to be here.

i never expected to get this old. i don't know why i survived all the beatings and my mother trying to kill me all the accidents all the adventures all the pain all the suffering. i wasn't trying to survive. i was trying to die.

i expected to die.

and yet death wouldn't take me and i was too stubborn to stay down to just stop to just kill myself. but no one especially not when i'm walking with the black dog can convince me that i deserve to be alive that i deserve to live or that i have a future that i want to be in a tomorrow a tomorrow that i want to be a part of.

i cannot say this out loud to a professional because they'll interpret it as me being suicidal and lock me up in a system where i get no help i just get locked away with other sad and crazy people because society still does not know what to do with us but the real reason the great reason for my depression is that i'm still alive. no medicine no therapy and nothing anyone can do can get the beast of a black dog off of me.

and so i live with the black dog until he decides to go away.

if he decides to go away.

he has been with me a lot this winter.

and he is growing larger and larger.

he wants me to kill myself.

he wants me to end it.

he almost won last year.

but i am too stubborn to let him win.

the black dog is on me again.

he has very sharp teeth.

and he is very heavy.

he is no friend.

he is nothing like any other dog i have known.

all other dogs that i have known have been friends in one way or another.

he is not my friend.

but i know him well.

the black dog is relentless.

the black dog will never go away.

not for good.

i know the black dog too well.

today it seems he is all i know.

today it seems the black dog is all that there is.

today it seems that the black dog is all that there ever will be.

the black dog is on me again.

the black dog is with me again.

i have spent too much time with the black dog.

maybe tomorrow he will go away.

or the day after that.

but he'll be back.

he always comes back. he always comes back.

but so far and it has been many years the black dog has not won.

i am no easy opponent.

he will not win today.

no. the black dog will not win today.

i don't know about tomorrow.

but he will not win today.

isaac

god you were beautiful.

i remember when mom brought you home. i was at glenview
that week and i came home from school and i don't know if
i knew exactly your story then. i was so young. and you were
younger. and there you were standing in the living room. this
perfect little blond haired blue eyed child. you looked like a
doll. i don't know if i was truly overcome with joy and love at
that moment or i wanted mom and dalton who was the only
real father i ever knew to think that i was but i rushed over
to hug you which was a strange thing for me to do consid-
ering i didn't like being touched and i was clumsy i am clumsy
maybe i hugged you too hard or hit you by accident i don't
know but i remember that mom yelled at me and the next
day i was sent back to the reserve. i don't remember blaming
you but i do remember feeling time and time again that you
were being chosen over me not just by them. by everyone.
you were so beautiful and so full of joy and light. you were
good at everything and everyone loved you. i was awkward
and miserable and angry and so i tried to beat the beauty and
the grace out of you.

i rarely thought of you as adopted. you seemed to belong
to that family more than i did. but though i used the word
brother and i only used the word brother and i only use the
word brother when i talk about you i did not think of you
as my brother then but i just didn't have another word for

what you were to me and i never said it out loud at least i don't think that i did but i despised myself because you were everything that i wished i were including loved.

it seemed like everything came so easy to you. like you put on skates and you didn't just skate better than everyone else you flew like an angel on ice every move you moved was perfection hearing your skates cut the ice while i struggled and strained and i spent most of time with jack on the reserve even though he was hardly ever there. you and debby lived in the nice warm house in glenview which was government housing but so much nicer than anything i had ever known.

i did not know why nobody seemed to want me.

only years later would it occur to me that debby was never sent to the reserve because the reserve then was a terrible place for girls and there was jack and my uncles and fernand. i thought it was because i was not wanted by anyone. and maybe that was part of it because i was strange and angry and dirty and snot was always running from my nose while you were golden and beautiful and everyone loved you and debby was beautiful too and when i was brought back to glenview heights for those brief periods when they needed to prove to welfare that i lived there i spent almost all my time trying to destroy your golden beauty. and then when they moved to toronto because of mom's sickness they had to bring me because they were claiming me on child welfare and you and i were thrown in a room together and you were loved so loved and so beautiful and i was not and so i tried to make you ugly i beat on you and chipped away at you because he the man i called father dalton loved you so much and you were blond and golden and i was not and i hated you both for what you were and what i was not.

together with debby we did our best to break you to dirty you to make you not so golden.

i don't know if we succeeded but we never stopped trying.

i never stopped trying.

you were still you but you became for a time almost as angry and as bitter as i was. and then our roles reversed. i could act as the reasonable one. the good one. the one others admired and looked up to. even when you did all the work and were the one who was there i was the one who did not drink or smoke or do drugs. i was the one who did martial arts and mystical things. i was the smart one. and even you forgot that you always outsmarted me. i was just better at reading books and saying and writing things. that did not make me smarter than you that does not make me smarter than you it just makes me better at these things than you in the same way that you are better at so many things than me. you are still the one who is strong enough to try to make a family and be a father and a grandfather and a husband while i still wandered and wander aimlessly calling myself free but really being a coward not trusting myself not to be jack or my mother and knowing that i'm too selfish and lack the control to be a good or even a decent father or husband so i live the life of a stranger and let you and let debby try and by trying of course make mistakes. and i never am trying to seem to make no mistakes and seem blameless when really like jack like bob your real father who married my mother's sister and denied you were his son when jackie took her life and then married jack my blood father's sister darquise who drove even bob to kill himself i took no responsibility at all. i just did it in a way that seemed a noble choice. but really was a cowardly choice and i told myself i did no harm but i left so many scars on you and in you and i was not there for debby and for shawn and for tabitha and for tyler and in a different way for zach and for josh or for anyone that mattered in the family and i told myself and some said that's just the way that i was but i could have done so much better i should have done so much better starting with how i was with you and then you wonder and others wonder why you are so angry maybe you think it is your inheritance it is in your blood but i remember that it was not how you started in the world not who you started out to be. and you hear about me and you look at me and you probably want to scream at others that i am not good. i am just fooling people the way that jack fooled people and i wanted to scream at them when they told me what a good man he was and maybe i and maybe debby are not the only reasons but isaac you were a happy innocent golden child and i hope you have moments of happiness now more than moments of sadness. you have a good wife and a family and you are a grandfather now and i am so sorry for the part that i played in making you more like the rest of us i really am i was and am a terrible big brother but i am your brother and i do love you i really do. but now i am so broken that i am afraid to let you or anyone i love be close to me for more than short brief periods for fear that i will bring my brokenness into your life and i stay away now not because i do not care but because i do so care and maybe that is just another excuse i have been making excuses for so long that i do not know anymore but i do love you and i am so sorry and i think about you often isaac even if i am absent in body i am never absent in thought or in love though those are the easy things i cannot say it enough i love you brother i love you isaac and i am so sorry for what i did to you and what i did not do for you.

you were so beautiful.

you were such a happy child.

maybe in our world you were doomed to become something else.

but in my pain and in my anger i set out to make you less golden.

less happy.

and i and our world did so much damage.

i set out to hurt you and i did.

i set out to make you less beautiful.

i set out to make you less golden.

i set out to make you more like me.

and i did all those things.

and for that for so many things i am so sorry.

i am so sorry.

i hope you are happy now.

i hope that your children and your grandchildren know that you are still golden.

that you are still beautiful.

i know that we were not raised to believe that men should be called beautiful or thought of as beautiful. maybe you will settle for golden. because that is what you were that is what you are.

a golden child a golden man.

that is what dad saw.

that is what i saw.

that is what i tried to destroy.

because i was jealous.

because i am jealous.

because i was not golden and you are you are golden.

brother. my golden brother.

isaac.

i am sorry.

and i love you.

it is not enough.

it is not nearly enough. but it is all that i have left to offer.

isaac.

i love you.

kaniatarowanenneh

i see you a small child by the kaniatarowanenneh the river. you sit on the rocks among the reeds and you are not happy you do not know how to be happy but you are at peace. i do not know that place.

i do not know peace.

you are not on the island. not on the akwesasne cornwall island but perhaps somewhere else on the reserve though perhaps not. you walk a lot. great distances. perhaps the place is at long sault or in the other direction towards st. regis. it is a hidden place. a simple place. but for you not like any other place.

you sit there for hours just listening to the river watching the seaweed the occasional fish and crayfish. the birds. the muskrats and other small animals. the river. your tóta your grandmother calls the river kaniatarowanenneh but you have always called it the st. lawrence named after a saint who supposedly was roasted to death and said i am cooked on one side turn me over. maybe the settlers named it after him because the mohawks and the hurons the kanien'kehá:ka and the wyandot were known for cooking people and sometimes eating them though that had more to do with taking their victim's power and sending their body into the next life without it. the algonquins called your grandmother's people mohawk which means maneater though some of them did the same thing but the kanien'kehá:ka heard it and thought it would make many others afraid and so took it as their own.

we tell stories by repeating them. by saying things over and over again.

your grandfather and your father were kanien'kehá:ka as well but only your tóta lived the life of a kanien'kehá:ka lived a life that honored the ancestors and so you only think of her as one of them. she taught you some of the old ways and your friend roger did too but your mother was white and your clan is decided by your mother and your membership in the tribe could not happen even though some strings were pulled back then and you lost your status in the tribe when you left the reserve when you were only 12 and though your soul feels kanien'kehá:ka you are embarrassed now to make that claim though you lived on the reserve when living there was very hard and you earned your claim by suffering all that suffering your mother is not what she should have been and you cannot make that claim and you do not look the look and so how dare you make the claim and so you sit and you listen to the river because the river does not judge you the river knows you for who you are and that you belong here and that you fit in this place and when they take you away from here how will your heart how will your soul how will your spirit survive.

but you will always know the river.

you are so young and yet you have already died so many deaths. you are so young and yet you are already so old. your spirit is as old as the river. your wounds are as old as the river. your scars are as old as the river.

they have tried to remake the river. to tame it. they build locks and dams to make it safe for ships and they tamed its rapids but it remembers that it is still the mighty river even if it is not as wild anymore even if it is scarred and wounded and caged it remembers that it is the mighty river and you can hear the majesty still in its voice even if the world does not fear it and does not honour it the way that it once did. you can feel the majesty still in its soul and in its spirit. and you love listening to it speak because its voice is ancient and wise and mighty and your ancestors listened to it for generations.

when you first come to sit here by kaniatarowanenneh you are angry. it takes some time but you forget to be angry. your family is good at anger. your family is so good at rage. even the women do not do sad and so you are all angry. you are all rage machines. but when you are here by the river in this place you have hidden even from your future self you are not angry and you are not sad. you just sit with the river. perhaps she is your greatest friend and you do not have many friends. you never will. but the friends you make you love deeply and you will never forget them and that includes kaniatarowanenneh she will stay with you all of your life you will hold her in your heart and in your spirit and this place by kaniatarowanenneh will stay with you inside of you even when you are at your darkest even when the black dog is right on top of you this place will be there kaniatarowanenneh will be with you as all your friends will be with you in your heart and in your soul because you are a loyal friend. many bad things can be said about you later but never that you are not a loyal friend and your friends are loyal and your love and their love will remain as long as you live perhaps even longer than that perhaps as long as kaniatarowanenneh flows.

she is a loyal friend and she will not forget you.

you come to the river to this spot when it is storming and when it is bitter cold. when the river is completely frozen over and when she is raging. she is still kaniatarowanenneh and she is still your friend and you know her and she knows you and your bond remains the same.

you will go back to her as an adult though never to that spot because the adult will never know where that spot was or even if it still exists. what matters is that she still exists that the river still exists that kaniatarowanenneh still exists and that spot still exists in the adult's mind in the adult's heart in the adult's soul that you still exist. and that is what matters in the end.

i see you.

that little boy.

that old little boy.

i feel you.

you are a part of me.

and kaniatarowanenneh is a part of me.

at times you seem far away.

at times she seems far away.

that place seems so far away.

that still quiet place.

but you are not. she is not. that place is not.

i carry you with me.

i carry her with me.

i carry it with me.

you.

the river.

the place.

i see you.

i feel you.

i know you.

and i will know you.

and i will know her.

always.

tricksters

there have been many tricksters in my life.

there have been so many tsó:ka'we nikakwaho'tà:a and tehahonhtané:ken crows coyotes and rabbits in my life.

i have not always taken notice.

i have not always know them for what they were because they can trick you into thinking they are something else.

dr. seuss and his love of nonsense may be the first writer that i remember who danced with tricksters though roger my tóta and others on the reserve told me many stories that taught my mind to circle and dance and wind in among the trees as well as not know where i was going some of the time how to get joyfully lost and blissfully in trouble. they conjured worlds for me and i conjured worlds from them and still i conjure them and still they conjure me the storytellers and the mystics and the dreamers and the poets the tsó:ka'we and nikakwaho'tà:'a and tehahonhtané:ken and mockingbird and tsitotsheriné:ken the nightingale. they float through my mind through my spirit through my many years of being the most unwanted child i or anyone i knew could imagine but there were the ancestors running through me because for me as a child then and even somewhat now the material world and the spiritual world were not divided and the pain of the residential schools and the love of an elder for her people and there were ghosts and there were spirits and the dances around a thousand fires and the voices of a thousand councils

and they ran through me they run through me and there was
emily dickinson and william blake and faulkner and eleanor
roosevelt and gandhi and maya angelou and more than i can
name and they taught me to dream they taught me to let my
mind reach and circle and tsó:ka'we and nikakwaho'tà:a and
tehahonhtané:ken they play their games their trickster games
shadows dancing around the fires shadows dancing in my
mind on my spirit inviting me to dance with madness again
and again and sometimes i'm afraid that i'm dancing too close
to my mother's madness and sometimes i am reminded that i
do not dance with the crazy tricksters and their funny games
and force me to pay attention and force me to remember who
i am and where i come from and who i come from and that
the mother the great mother who made everything is not
just love she is not just easy she is challenge and she is tricks
and tricksters and she is death as well as life and she dances
around a fire that will burn you that will blind you that will
choke you with its ashes even while it is warming you and
giving you light and giving you life and she put tsó:ka'we and
nikakwaho'tà:a and tehahonhtané:ken here to play with us
and to trick us and sometimes to do things that we think are
terrible because we do not understand that to them it is all
a game and there is no malice and cruelty there is only their
nature the nature of the trickster that knows only that this
is all a game not a cruel game or a good game or a bad game
just a game and they try to trick because that is what they do.

i'd go to east front school in the city and come back across
the river to the reserve thinking that the world worked in
straight lines but sooner or later tsó:ka'we or nikakwaho'tà:a
or tehahonhtané:ken would come into my brain into my
spirit and tell me that all that was all that is moves in circles
in never ending spirals in repetitions in constant and never
ending repetition and stories that get told over and over and
over again and the white half of me wanted the straight lines
stories to have a beginning and an end and to have some

kind of obvious meaning because they made more sense they
could be understood because things came to a beginning and
end but the tricksters kept telling the indian half of me that's
what they called it then that there were no beginnings and
no ends there was only endless transformation and when
the white part of me tried to make sense of this it couldn't
it defied reason and nikakwaho'tà:'a laughed and tsó:ka'we
laughed and tehahonhtané:ken laughed just because we
want it to make sense does not mean it has to make sense
and just because we want to create lines and divisions does
not mean they actually exist it is a quantum universe where
the cat is alive and not alive and particles are entangled and
there is dark matter and dark energy and indians that's what
we called ourselves then have always known that we gather
in circles around fires and know of the scared spirit wheel
and the sacred spiral because tsó:ka'we and nikakwaho'tà:a
and tehahonhtané:ken and other tricksters will always
be there have always been there to knock things from any
straight line off balance to keep the world from being straight
and easy and predictable and boring they will sneak up on
you and pull your pants down they will trip you just when
you think you have balance they will get you lost from the
path that you know and you expect and maybe you will be
wounded or injured maybe you will die or maybe you will
discover something brand new or that you lost or that you
didn't know you had lost or was missing that could not have
been found until you got lost until you fell down and my
tóta and roger and all the storytellers and the music and the
dances told me never to ignore tsó:ka'we or nikakwaho'tà:a
or tehahonhtané:ken or any trickster not just because they
are dangerous they are dangerous but because they are
important they are essential they made the world and human
beings and they remind us that the world is on a'nó:wara's
turtle's back it is not flat or straight and when you forget
that or convince yourself that there is straight lines and flat

surfaces the tricksters will always remind you one way or the other that there is not and you can listen to them you can play with them or you can fight them and even if you somehow win what good is life if there are no surprises no tricks no laughter no nikakwaho'tà:'a and no tsó:ka'we and no tehahonhtané:ken.

some days i forget that we need the surprises the tricks the laughter.

it is good to have é:rhars to have dogs around because they always have some coyote in them especially when they are up to no good. it is good to listen to tsó:ka'we's laughter their caw caw caw as they sit up in the trees and laugh at us because we cannot fly among other things that tsó:ka'we finds so funny. it is good to see tehahonhtané:ken every now and then with her ears perked up and her nose smelling the air ready to crawl under anything and pass any border that we create. it is good to know that the tricksters are still there.

it is good even though when we create walls and borders to keep them out even when we try to chase them away they are there and whether we see them or not they are ready to trip us to trick us and to show us that what we thought we knew what we thought was real and solid and straight the ground that we thought was so so solid is not it has never been and when we think we cannot fall is when we are the most easy to trip to trick and nothing is as real or as solid as we think it is and if we forget that then we will get a visit from tsó:ka'we or nikakwaho'tà:a or tehahonhtané:ken or some other trickster and we can fall or we can leap we can try to hold on or we can let go we can scream in fear or frustration or we can laugh because no matter what we do to the trickers we are laughable we are two legged hairless absurd animals that think because we think we are special that think because we think because we depend so much on that we do think we have some god or something that we treat like it is a god to worship and above all to worship reason we are beyond the reach of all that is natural but we are reminded again and again by earthquakes and weather and disease that we are no more beyond reach and yet still we convince ourselves that we have mastered the world but nikakwaho'tà:'a and tsó:ka'we and tehahonhtané:ken and the other trickers are there to remind us that we are not masters of anything we are just the only animal that is stupid enough to think that we possibly could be and that makes us laughable the most laughable of all because we are the only animals that see the world as we want it to be not as it is and so we go on willfully blindered and so many of us do not see the tricksters and do not see that it does not matter if you see the tricksters or not they are there.

and we can live with them and laugh with them or we can pretend that they do not exist that the world is what we want it to be rather than what it is and not only will we continue to fall but we will drag others with us we will continue to make this world a hell by trying to make it a garden controlled and tidy world rather than a real messy sometimes frightening world by building walls and borders and more illusions acting as tricksters upon ourselves by becoming the cruelest kind of trickster with no humour and no playfulness just a spoiled child's will that things are as we wish they are.

i have had many tricksters in my life.

many nikakwaho'tà:'a.

many tsó:ka'we.

many tehahonhtané:ken.

i am very thankful that they were there.

i am thankful that they are there sometimes i forget to laugh.

sometimes i forget to play.

i am old now and in great pain.

i have lived a life that has to be paid for.

that is no excuse.

the tricksters are still there.

they invite me to play.

they invite me to laugh.

some days i remember to look for them.

some days i do not.

i am only half indian after all.

half of me knows that tsó:ka'we is always there.

half of me knows that nikakwaho'tà:'a is always there.

half of me knows that tehahonhtané:ken is always there.

but even that half of me forgets sometimes.

even that half of me starts to think the world works in straight lines.

and then none of me is indian.

that's what we called ourselves when i grew up.

and then i fall down.

i've forgotten how to fall it hurts more than it used to.

but then something makes me laugh.

or i hear a tsó:ka'we laughing to another crow.

or i see tehahonhtané:ken up to no good.

or maybe nikakwaho'tà:'a if i'm really lucky.

and then i remember.

i remember who i am.

i remember what i am.

i just remember.

and memory is the best trick of all.

it makes you forget who you are today.

and remember who you were yesterday.

that's quite a trick sometimes if you ask me.

quite a trick to play on yourself if you ask me.

sometimes you can be the best trickster of them all.

sometimes you can play tricks on you without even knowing you are doing it.

that makes you a pretty good trickster if you ask me.

maybe the best trickster of them all.

occupation

i have an occupation of violence.

i have made a preoccupation with violence.

i cannot remember when i started fighting and i cannot remember my life without fighting without violence at its core.

i was lucky enough that roger gave me direction by getting involved in martial arts and boxing and wrestling at a very young age. i didn't need to learn them to know how to fight. i needed to learn them to know how not to fight. they taught me and roger taught me and my many senseis and sifus and trainers taught me discipline and a sense of responsibility and respect. similarly with hunting and trapping something that roger also taught me. it came with deep respect and honour for your prey and roger taught me that when i no longer had to hunt and trap to eat i had to stop killing and i did.

and with horses and dogs. there too is respect and discipline. and empathy. how to listen with your whole body not with just your ears as with hunting but here to cooperate with another living being. but that too could end in violence if not done right.

and i continued to fight because fighting was what i knew. it was at the core of who i was but more and more the fighting was in the defense of others and it never was for me an attempt to prove anything. because i knew that jack my blood father and so many others in my family were geniuses of violence but that did not make them men and that certainly did not make them warriors anymore than it did me. though i certainly made no attempt to rob others of their illusions or their delusions about me and about my family and our capacity for violence and how that made us in their eyes brave and strong and something to be admired. i most certainly allowed them their illusions and their delusions about that. i had my ego and perhaps i started to believe that i was this mystical warrior monk billy jack bruce lee figure that so many saw me as. i definitely believed i was at times. though the broken me the me that had never known any kind of love from any kind of parent still lingered inside of me and knew yes knew that i was not worthy of any kind of love or respect or admiration of any kind which is why i pushed people away which is why i never allowed them to get too close to me because they would see that and know yes know that i was despicable yes despicable as the child me had been taught by so many by almost the entire world that i was despicable and did not do not belong on this earth.

i have never known how to love me because the child did not think that he was loved but he was i was and i always have been loved there was always there is always a tóta or a roger or a laura or someone who has loved me despite myself despite my hatred yes my hatred for myself my loathing my deep loathing yes it goes beyond hatred and yet and yet i have been loved i am loved and i have loved and i do love beyond all reason beyond all that i know yes know or think that i know about myself i am i was i have always been loved and i am and i was and i have always been loving this i know to be true this i know to be true in the darkness in my darkest moments there is that this flickering light this also light that will not go out that will not go away despite despite despite all that i think that i know despite the black dog no matter how big he grows no matter how he sinks his teeth into my bones and my path of violence of controlled violence became somehow one of advocation not just vocation but yes of advocation and not just occupation but a kind of vocation and even at times a sublimation that i who did not want to live and who did not care about the well being of my body or of any part of me began to in small ways put those things put myself in the way of harm to others i who had never run from trouble began to run towards trouble and i who was good at so very good at violence i had joined the army and instead of learning a trade like sensible people i learned how to jump out of planes and shoot people and that made me more good at violence and then i went to university and i studied psychology and minored in theatre and learned not how people think but to think about how people think and changed my minor to physiology to know how the body worked and i trained people trained fighters and was a bouncer in some of the toughest clubs in the city and i could get someone out of a bar without a single punch being thrown but if it came down to that i could go toe to toe with bikers and gang members and i faced people with knives and guns and broken bottles and i became a legend for how good i was at spotting trouble before it started and i became a peacemaker more than a fighter more and more i used what i knew about the way people work to avoid violence and prevent and protect in my own small way and then more and more friends started dying being shot and i knew it was time to get out because no matter how good you are a gun is all it takes and i began to train and to teach and still i followed the path more and more alone though there was always those that grew close despite me i lost so many and i did not know how to be with an other in the way that people are with each other perhaps the asperger's definitely the asperger's but also the core of self loathing that remained no matter how much i was loved and that i loved though my mind began to know that i was worthy there was that child that unloved despised despicable child and he would not he could not be denied and i lived despite myself and loved despite myself and was

loved despite myself because in the end though i was jack
delorme's i am jack delorme's child i am more than that i am
more than my mother's sickness and more than the horrors of
my childhood there was there is something that my tóta that
roger that laura and so many others saw inside me something
decent something that wanted to be decent something that
wants to be decent that wants to be a proud member of my
tribe something that goes beyond and above all the wrong
that was done to me because there was good done for me as
well and that too lives in me like a small miracle it lives and it
grows and it goes on and i have fed it and nurtured it with the
things that i have done and the things that i have learned and
while there is so much darkness there is that little miracle
that has grown and grown and survived inside me and been
nurtured by others by so many others more than i can even
name and perhaps compared to other lives it may not seem
much or anything at all but for me for me it is a thing i do
not have the words for but i know i know when there is the
deepest darkness when the black dog has his teeth sunk deep
into me i know that this little light this little miracle is there
and maybe it is not much but it makes me yes it makes me
worthwhile it makes me worthwhile though i often do not
believe that there it is and i do know it i know it and there are
so many i have to thank for it and i am glad that i myself have
nurtured it and some days it is what i hold onto it is all that i
hold onto and i sometimes i often have to remind myself it is
there but my occupation has become has become

remembering

and knowing

that i am also

this little light.

that i am more than the sum of my darkness.

that i am somehow more.

káryo

you are that other boy.

káryo.

the wild one.

the angry one.

you do not wait by the river you do not stand anywhere peacefully. though sometimes you perch on a ridge where you can see clearly what is coming. for the most part you are all movement. you are all energy. you are all wildness and rage. and you too want to be heard and want to be seen. but you frighten me. you are what i think i left behind what i tried to leave behind. what i tried to bury.

and you will not be tamed. you are my enkidu my esau and edom and my káryo though you are not hairy and you are not my bother you are the wild boy the wild thing that lives inside of me and would be heard. you are not easy like the boy by the river you are all pain and rage but you are there and need to be heard and to be seen. you are the wild boy that i left behind that i hid from and more and more as i grew older and strove to be less violent. i tried to bury you.

i feared you. i fear you. you are what i have been taught is wrong with me. it is wrong to be angry. pain is to be avoided like anger. and the wildness in me that was such a big part of who i was when i was living on the reserve but was something to be tamed when i moved to the city and you were to be stuffed down and buried.

it is never said it is never ever but we hear we learn that
indigenousness is the opposite of intelligence because it is the
opposite of being civilized of progress and growth and so kill
the indian is no longer said but we grow up knowing that it is
meant that we cannot be indigenous and move forward at the
same time we cannot be indigenous and be considered intelligent since the sciences and technologies are the opposite
thing and so we must choose to go backwards or to push who
we are down and so kill the indian becomes the unspoken
truth that we learn without words and more and more as i
became educated and civilized and colonized i moved away
from you most of all because you were all that i thought was
wrong about me and i left you in the forest somewhere in the
forest and i added to your hurt and your anger by leaving you
behind by abandoning you though that little boy that káryo
is a part of me i denied yes i denied that you were a part of
me that you were me. and there you were so small and so
hurt and so angry and over time i buried you because i did
not want to be hurt i did not want to be angry i did not want
to be wild i did not want to be káryo a wild creature i did not
want to be a savage and i took the colonizer's definition of
what civilized of what learned of what intelligent was i took
their definition though i knew i knew that what they called
civilized was an equivocation what they called civilized really
meant the destruction and the undermining of all that did
not fit their values and that this kind of civilized i knew even
then was not civilized at all but they had made the rules and
they had made the definitions and you though you were only
a boy you were an abomination an abnegation to their civil-
ization to those definitions which without even the thought
was incorporated without conscious choice as my own rules
and definitions and so you were placed under a mound under
a great burial mound of some sort piled with stones of my
own making inside of me and abandoned and ignored which
was the very thing the source of your pain and your anger

and i am so sorry i am so very sorry that i did this to you child i did this too without even the thought of doing it but i did it nonetheless. and sometimes we commit the greatest evil without even the thought of committing the thing. and maybe the language which you knew has disappeared or became is becoming hidden they do not say indian and they do not say savage or any of those things they said to you at least not in public but the thought the belief has not changed instead the adult you the me of you hears we do not pay taxes or for university and we have casino money the same old tired and lazy complaints that have taken the place of the overt racism the out in the open hatred like all those things makes our lives so easy makes all the problems the generations of abuse the memories of kill the indian go away no no they still linger even if not said and i tell myself that i have moved on from you from that world that once existed but you are still very much a part of me no matter how i ignore no matter how thick the walls of the mound no matter how deep i think i've buried you you have not gone away you cannot go away you were made and you exist and you need me to come to you and listen to you to see you because you are angry for a reason your hurt comes from things that happened that were done to you to me and the world that you lived in that i lived in and that i still live in. i need to go back into the forest and find you and be with you and perhaps at first you'll scream and you'll flail at me at the world because that is what you need to do but you will not make me do bad things. that time has passed. i have to trust that the time has passed. and i just need to hear you and see you i need to be with you and let your hurt and your rage come out until we find out what is on the other side of that and i find out who you are beyond your anger and your hate and beyond my fear of you this boy this other child this káryo who has been buried who has been silenced for who knows how many years. i need to know you this other this lost this káryo this wild boy.

i need to learn to love you.

you are not easy to love as i was not easy to love as i am not easy to love.

i tell myself i have told myself that the best things in life are not easy in the same way the great poetry and great art is not easy. in the way life is not easy. in the way the universe is not easy. in the way that nature is not easy. but i have hidden from you and i have hidden you from me because you are not easy. you are no garden with tidy walls nice and neat you are wild you are kárуo you are unkempt and messy you are what they used to call savage though they would never use that word now and for so long i have feared your wildness your volatility and what you might do if i set you loose and so i buried you and did my best to forget that you existed but you are not just wild not just kárуo you are the kanien'kehá:ka the haudenosaunee the indigenous the ancestors who would be called wild and savage by the colonizers and the little boy who sits by the river he is the acceptable part of that in me but you you are the part of me that will not be tamed that will not be colonized. and the more i turned away from you the more white i became. i could smudge and spirit walk and learn the words again but that part of me that defiant part of me that is angry because he is supposed to be angry is hurt because he is supposed to be hurt because he has been hurt and you are more angry now and you are more hurt now and you are angry at me and you are hurt by me because i left you i left i abandoned you how dare i when i know what that means what it is to be abandoned and when i begin to remove the rocks when i begin to remove the stones that i put between us i hear you i feel you raging from the other side and i want to stop oh how i want to stop but i will not i will not there are many stones there is so much between us i'm surprised you are still there i tried to kill you yes i tried to kill you i thought it better that you did not exist at all but now but now you are still there still you stand and you rage and your rage is earned your rage is earned and when all of the stones are gone you will no doubt scratch at my eyes and punch and kick and bite me and you will be hard to contain káryo but you deserve to be free and you do not just deserve to be free i need you to be free i need you káryo inside of me to remind me of who i am and what i come from and who i come from.

we are not separate. no matter what i tried to do. no matter what i tried to do to you we have never been and we will never be separate. we are one thing you and i. we are one thing but we are not whole. it will take time and it will take great effort and it will be painful and it will be frightening but i will do it i will do it and i will hear your voice káryo and i will feel your hurt and i will feel your fury but i am large i am much larger now than i was i can contain all of that and i can know all of that without it breaking me and i will know you for all that you are as you are as you were and as you will be. and i cannot say that i do not fear you i have only tasted the wild in many years and you are nothing but káryo you are nothing but wild you are not a thing to be caged or walled and i have sinned against myself by trying to do these things to you and trying to kill you not in that christian sense that confession and penance can undo or merely loving something that is so insecure that it requires your love before it can love you back all of those things must be done or undone as the case might be but they will not be merely enough i will feel your fury and your pain and i will know it. i must know it. and perhaps there is no end to those things. but perhaps if i stand and i bear and i know what these things that i have done to you have caused perhaps on the other side there will be a knowing of you as you were not as you are as a child of the wilderness as káryo. i will know you i will not hold you because you do not want to be held but perhaps i will finally see you and i will finally know you.

i don't know what that will mean.

i don't know what will happen.

i just know that little boy must be found again.

i just know káryo must be found again.

the other little boy.

the lost little boy.

the buried little boy.

the wild little boy.

he too must be seen.

he too must be heard.

káryo.

i am coming for you.

there are so many stones.

so many stones and i have put them there.

but i am coming for you.

shape shifter

i have been a shape shifter.

when i was a boy i wanted to tell all the people all the many people that told me that my blood father was a good man that he wasn't a good man that he had tricked them that he was a monster and he was only pretending to be good man. i would have told them that as awkward and as unlikable as i was as i am at least i was who i was but something kept me quiet maybe that it would do no good or maybe i was keeping his secret for my own sake because the one thing i did not want do not want the world to see me as is a victim.

and so i was never who i was no matter how i told myself that i was.

or maybe i stayed silent because deep down i suspected that the monster that i knew was not the whole man not the entire story and i wanted it to be simple because in order to hate someone or something we have to make the story simple so i could not allow the thought that maybe there was a good man in him and i just was one of the things that brought out the monster not that it was my fault but that my very existence was a kind of trigger to the monster in jack.

i never physically or even verbally abused children or women except for isaac but i gave myself permission to let that monster out in certain circumstances and on men that were big enough or had the ability to defend themselves but the monster came out in other ways too. my brother isaac couldn't defend himself for most of his life when i took my rage out on him when we moved to toronto and i did not want to be there even though it wasn't his fault my sister and i took a happy and joyous little boy and tried to turn him into an angry man.

meanwhile i took the skills that roger and my tóta had taught me to hide my asperger's that's what they called it then to seem like a calm and rational one in my family. i hid my rage for years by taking it out on isaac and getting in fights for what seemed like good reasons. i never drank or did drugs and i stayed out of jail and told myself that i was better than jack better than the rest of my family and even they believed it until isaac and those that really knew me wanted to tell people that i wasn't such a great guy that i really wasn't and in a different way i had become jack.

when i was 16 i ran off and joined the army with a stolen id so they wouldn't know how old i really was and that too convinced everybody that i was so clean cut and good the image everyone has of the military but i joined so that i could practice how to do horrible things beside horrible racist drunken people. not all of them. just the ones that i was drawn to. but when i was discharged i did finish high school and went to university to study psychology of all things on the army's dime and i also used years of martial arts and boxing wrestling training to make money as a fighter and a bouncer the truth was not only did i enjoy hurting but i enjoyed being hurt not as a sexual thing but because pain was so familiar and seemed right to me and i remembered someone once asking jack why he was so mean to me and him saying because that's all he's good for.

that's all that i was good for.

and i grew my hair long again and i wrote poetry and i became an actor and a playwright and i joined a band and because i was artistic and people especially women saw me as special i was always so gentle with them that they fell in love with me and then i left them my acts of violence were emotional not physical because they always thought it was their fault when i left them but i hurt so many people there were so many casualties of my hidden rage the hidden monster in me and i blamed it all on my abusive childhood on growing up on a reserve and in the shadow of the residential school though my friends and i would look at each other when we'd hear an indian that's what we called it then even stub his toe and blame it on the white man and we would roll our eyes and though i left when i was twelve and the only time i really thought about the half of me that was mohawk that was kanien'kehá:ka was when i visited roger who moved to the reservation on salt river in arizona and he made me remember the best of my spirit and the monster seemed far away and then i would go back to my life and the monster would creep back in and i hurt so many people that were better than me. they deserved better than me. and i walked away from so much so many people tried to give me a future so many believed in me but i knew i did not deserve to be happy i had never been happy because all i was good for was to take it take the violence take the suffering that's what i was here for and maybe in the beginning that was other people's fault but then it became my own fault and i had to become my own skinwalker my own shape shifter.

and i went on trying on different shapes i became a trainer a teacher a candlestick maker and i told myself and let others believe that i was who i was. i excused my rage as a tool like everything else. i was so good at what i did that people saw only the shape and thought i was the best of the best some-one something to emulate to admire but really the monster was becoming so heavy that i could no longer carry him yet still i carried on shifting shapes leaving behind myths and damage that i was rarely blamed for until the only person that i could damage was myself and i found myself old older than my years much older than i ever expected to be and falling down i cannot walk sometimes i cannot get out of bed and still i blame other monsters not the one inside me and i avoid mirrors and cameras because this is not a shape that i choose it is a shape that has chosen me and whereas for so long the monster inside me could hide behind the beauty of youth now there is nothing to hide behind and just an old sad man looking back at me and he is still angry though he doesn't remember why there is no one left to blame though he still blames those old long dead monsters that weren't monsters at all just human beings and he doesn't know how to be just a human being he has been shifting shapes so long that he doesn't know what he looks like he doesn't want to know what he really looks like so he so i hide from mirrors and cameras i hide from myself and i have done for so long i don't know how to stop changing shape.

people say to me what a great person that i am or i was and i want to scream at them that i'm tricking them that i'm a monster that i don't even know how to be human being all that i know is how to be a lightning rod for other people's and even my own hate and anger and so that's all that i've ever really been good for.

i'm not a human being.

i'm a shape shifter.

maybe that's all i've ever been.

maybe that's all i'll ever be.

a thing that brings an action.

a broke down shape shifter.

i've been doing it for so many years that i don't how to do anything else.

i have been a shape shifter so that even i do not know who or what i really am.

and the real truth the terrible truth is that i am what i have been hiding from. what i have been hiding from is not what i really am or what i have really become but from what i have not become what promises i have failed to live up to that like my sister debby and like so many people perhaps like nearly all people i am not who i set out to be i am not who i was meant to be.

i have used the hardship and poverty and the abuse and so many other things that happened to me but have not made me and have not broken me at least not completely as the excuses not to be what my tóta saw and roger saw and goat saw and trooper saw and maybe later laura saw underneath and others saw glimpses of because that person could feel hurt could feel pain could feel loss and so many other things so it was better to pretend to be people who weren't real to shape shift from one to the other when the going got rough or i came to close to feeling anything.

i know who i was meant to be.

i know what i was supposed to be. i know that for certain.

i see the boy sitting by the river waiting for me.

i know that káryo the wild boy is waiting for me.

i contain multitudes. they sit near the center of that circle by the sacred fire waiting for me to see them to acknowledge that they are all there.

and now all that i have to do is to take one step one step towards them one step in the world that we call real without shifting my shape.

and then another.

put one foot in front of the other. and just be.

just be. it sounds so easy.

it is not easy.

it is the most difficult thing that i have ever done.

but i am trying to do it.

there is fear and uncertainty.

the boy sits waiting for me. by the kaniatarowanenneh.

by the river.

in that still secret place.

the others wait for me too.

káryo waits for me.

buried beneath all the stones.

and i can hear kaniatarowanenneh.

i can feel otsénha.

i can feel the fire.

that they have gathered around.

but i have to come to otsénha as a being.

not as a doing or a thing waiting for something to be done to it.

just be.

i cannot lie to those by kaniatarowanenneh.

i will not lie to those around otsénha.

because the place by kaniatarowanenneh.

by otsénha is truth.

perhaps the boy and káryo and i will sit by that rock by the kaniatarowanenneh.

perhaps the boy will finally show us where his secret place is.

and together we will just he and the two of us will just be.

and the others.

the others that i have loved.

the others that have loved me.

they wait for me too.

but first i have to choose a shape.

just one shape.

and be that one shape.

stop being a shape shifter.

until then.

until then nothing new can really happen.

it sounds so easy.

it sounds so easy.

to stop shifting shapes.

just stop.

it sounds so easy.

so why

oh why

does it feel

so very

very

impossible to me.

so very

impossible to be.

dalton

you dalton lauber are my real father.

the man i will always think of as father the man i too
often refer to as my step father. you were not as big and
as handsome or as admired by as many as my blood father
jack. and you were not always kind to me and you did not
always understand me. nobody did. i did not. i do not even
understand me. but you tried you really tried to love me and
my sister and my brother though none of us were actually
your children by blood and you loved my mother though she
was so hard to love. all of us were so hard to love and you
stayed and you fed us even when sometimes you could not
afford to feed yourself and you clothed us even when you
would walk around in the same worn out patched clothes.
and you dalton lauber were a man. you were my father you
were our father and i loved you even when i hated you. i love
you now for trying to love me when i was so hard to love
and my brother isaac was so easy to love. so i tried to beat
the beauty out of him because i wanted my father to love me
more to understand me more but by the time you knew me
maybe before that i was so broken and damaged so defective
that all you could do was try and you tried so hard you tried
so very hard.

i thought you were mean.

i thought you were harsh.

i thought you were just another white man.

i thought you were a racist.

you were a white man of german farmer stock and you were a racist in that way that people of your generation were racist. my mother was a racist too and she had married an indian that's what we called them then and had indian children. but that indian man had beaten her and abandoned her and his family had shunned her and so her racism seemed to make sense to me though she didn't just hate indians she hated black people and jewish people and anyone who was not what she considered white. but you my father my step father would call me names like wagon burner and warhoop as a joke but you never called my sister who was my blood father's child as well such names because she did not look as much like jack as i did and she had lived with you in cornwall so you my father or my step father as i thought of you then as just a white man calling me racist names and making racist jokes. and because we were poor we lived in housing projects where most of the people were black that's what they called it then well that's what they called it when they were being nice they and she and you had far worse words most of the time and you and my mother had never seen any real black people and you said terrible things about them because you had been raised to believe those things and that made me want to make friends with only black kids who wondered why this white kid that's what they saw wanted to be friends with them but i did not think i was white and i had grown up hating white people. you my father who i then called my step father were white. my brother looked as white as white could be.

even though he really wasn't. bob his father who isaac never even knew was his father was half cherokee but isaac was blonde haired and had blue eyes. and he did not see race his friends and girlfriends were black and white and everything in between. i hated him for that. how could he not see race.

how could skin colour not matter to him. i tried to beat that into him too.

mostly i hated him because you loved him so much.

the two of you are inseparable in my mind. inseparable in fact. as for you my father my step father i hated you for being white for bringing me to toronto for being a racist for not understanding me and for not loving me. the last two i didn't know i hated you for i hated the world in general for not understanding and not loving me but i hated you more because i thought that was supposed to be your job. my mother was mentally as well as physically ill so i felt like i could not blame her and i had developed a kind of stockholm syndrome relationship in my mind with jack so many people including you who were his friend told me what a great guy what a stand up guy he was and there was not enough distance yet for me to look at him clearly there is still not enough distance to see him clearly so surely i thought there was something wrong with me not him he said that's all i was good for was to be beaten and i believed him and yet i felt free to feel angry at you this white racist semi stranger. i can look back now and see that i was just as racist as you were. i did not use the words but i felt different about you because you were white and i hurt isaac because he looked white even though in reality i did too just not as much.

i can look back now and see how hard you tried to love me and that you were just a man of your time and place who spoke words that you had been taught but tried to overcome your beliefs when it mattered most. you came from a time and i came from a time when many men did not take responsibility for their children especially among the poor it was a joke that the definition of confusion on the reserve was father's day though i knew plenty of good fathers and even more good mothers on the reserve. most men on the reserve were not jack. most men were not jack. you stayed and took care of us even when there was no reward we hated you we were not his children and my mother raged at you and at the world and was supposed to die again and again we were all so difficult to love except isaac and we did our best to break him and i who did not know what it was to be loved who did not believe i was capable of being loved or that i was worthy of being loved i was good for only one thing i was so strange and so angry and so silent and so incapable of speaking words often stuttering and stammering when i did choose to speak and often saying the wrong words because of my dyslexia i who hated to be touched and to be even near others blamed you for not understanding and not loving me even though no one ever had even i did not even i do not even love myself i am a mystery i am a riddle to myself am hidden so much from myself yet i blamed you and i was angry at you because you found isaac so much easier to understand.

no one called me ishmael.

no one we grew up with would even get that joke.

they called me many other things but not that.

and then as i grew older and went out to live my life i stayed angry at you i was angry at everyone though in my mind i at least gave you credit for never physically abusing me or any of your children or your wife my mother though i remembered the shame of waking up with her on top of you beating you bloody and thinking it was because you were weak but you had made a rule that when you were drinking you would not hit anyone because you knew someone who had killed his child when he was drunk and you never hit my mother not ever but she only knew the abuse of jack and her father and maybe so many other men and so she too thought that made you weak that you would not hit her not even fight back when you both were drunk how much strength it must have taken to not hit back and she would hit everybody when she was drunk especially me because i reminded her of jack my

142

blood father and i would wake up with her with a knife i had become a light sleeper to stay alive from jack and from her and maybe i wanted you to do what i would never do to hurt her for trying to kill me so often and i spent the rest of my life trying to get myself killed but i was harder to kill than a russian monk i got into fights and i got shot at and stabbed and jumped off of things and i walked into wildernesses and deserts but i did not die and to actually commit suicide as so many in my family had was too much like giving up like taking a knee so i tried to get the world to do it but even death did not want me i went on despite no desire to actually go on and i took it out on everyone else and maybe i hated you because you were the one who did not try to kill me or maybe because you were the one who kept me alive when so many others wanted me dead including myself or maybe because you were decent to me and like my mother i was confounded by your decency and there was a space between the two of us that was different than the space between myself and everyone else and that space was not between you and isaac though it was there between debby my sister and you in a different way she wanted something from men that caused her pain and you were careful not to do that to her and like my mother and me she did not know how to bear decency. those who love us hurt us and because you did no harm refused to do harm it meant to us that you did not care.

and i grew older and i continued to be confounded by those who showed me kindness and decency and love there have been surprisingly many like my tóta roger and laura and many many others in fact too many others to list and i never could and i still cannot acknowledge that there must have that there must be something about me worthy of love and i was certainly not worthy of your love or at least not in my deepest heart and yet you did love me even so and i tried and tried but death did not want me though death had always walked so close to me and to my family and to those i knew

there were murders and suicides and accidents and sickness
that those close to me were swallowed by but never me never
me and i was confounded by that too because of all of them
i was the one who least wanted to be alive who would most
welcome and had most expected death for as long as i knew
and yet it took everyone around me to keep me alive and
those that it did not take i damaged most of all while seeming
so good and so decent i would hear them say i would see the
admiration in their eyes and i would think oh if they only
knew that i am the beast slouching off to bethlehem and that
even death will not have me i am a permanently damaged
child i am a wounded beast that for some reason will not die
and the only decent man the only decent human beings in
my life could not reach me and you the man who was my real
father because you took on the task and you raised me for no
reward i could not call you father like my sister would not
take your name only isaac did even though the name we hung
on to was of a man who did want us who in different ways
savaged our bodies and our souls as his own was savaged
and perhaps by his father and his father was by his father
before that by the schools and the church despite the fact
the fact that their people had never fought them and never
surrendered to them treated as prisoners as slaves as captives
and the true why of it long forgotten. not the facts. we know
the facts. the human why.

why do we do such things to each other time and time again
throughout history. why must human beings form lines
where there is a front and back those who lead and those who
they drag behind them instead of a circle where all are equal.
but the pain and the suffering passed on and down until they
until we knew nothing else and i hated you this white man
for being white despite the fact that you were kinder to me
than the man i called father and though my mother was white
and i did not hate her at least not in a way that i would allow
myself to know and i hated isaac for being blond haired and

blue eyed though his real father was half cherokee and i spent my life wanting to go back to the reserve despite the fact that except for my tóta and roger the reserve did not want me and barely knew me and my tóta was dead buried in a catholic cemetery which she would have hated and roger moved to the reservation on salt river there was nothing there for me except the river which i still loved which i still love but is so large and so old and so ever changing and there was this man who did the decent thing without who i may have lived but almost certainly would have lived a much darker life than the one i lived who became my example for whatever goodness there is in being a man and yet none of this none of this i gave back to you not even my mind and yet now that i am old somehow i managed to make it to old and you are gone when i think of you the love i feel is so great so large and so unspeakable that it feels as if i cannot bear it.

a certain grace has always come to me around death. i am hardly what would be considered a lucky man but in my later life some better angel has been there to allow me to do or to say those things that most others only wish they were allowed to do or say before a beloved soul passed on. i do not know why and i do not question why lest it cease to continue although perhaps there is only so much grace each person is granted but it has seemed the only aspect of my life where i've had anything like what others might call luck or grace.

in the case of you my father that grace was granted by my brother isaac who came into our lives like an angel and looked like a golden angel and who you were living with then because he was the only one of us who had a home and the ability and the will and the desire to care for you and it was always going to be he who would be caring for you. isaac let me know though he didn't have to that you didn't have much longer and had decided not to get any more treatment for the hepatitis that you had gotten from a syringe while fixing someone's plumbing because you always worked with your hands and isaac always worked with his hands while my hands were literally useless from the frostbite that i got on one of the rare occasions when i was in the city and two older boys beat me up because i was an indian and they didn't want me around their sister who i had made friends with and i could not wear my gloves because i was i am dyslexic and the fingers made no sense to me and no one knew i was dyslexic yet and i screamed that my hands were burning and the boys laughed because it was 20 below zero and how could my hands be burning when it was that cold and i came to the house in glenview with my hands swollen and black and jack was there to take me back to the reserve and he took me instead to cornwall general hospital and the doctor there saw jack saw that he was indian and said i should be taken to the hospital on the reserve and then when jack threatened to kill him the doctor wanted to amputate my hands but a korean doctor doctor kim told jack to take me to hotel dieu and he did and they saved my hands but i could not hold anything with my hands for years and my fingers were warped and even if that were not true i had no interest in what you did my mind was full of words and pictures and dreams not that i thought that working with my hands was beneath me i had done things with my hands like work with horses and other animals though it was very difficult with a weak grip and i admired and respected the work that you did and that isaac did and that others did it was honest work it builds and changes the world in a very literal way and repairs what is broken while so many others play with things that aren't real that don't really mean anything or do anything and yet they get paid well for it i just could not do what you did and what isaac does i did not have the aptitude i was nothing like you or anything that you knew so you and isaac were drawn together and one day the syringe the needle in some junkie's toilet and i went away as i do for years and in my head i think i believed you had already died but i was too afraid to fully think the thought and then isaac gave me the gift isaac gave me that gift of seeing you before you died.

i have a habit of just disappearing. maybe it's the asperger's or the years of isolation when i was a child or maybe i just run away from people. i never mean to it is never my plan to disappear or my conscious intention. but since i was a child i would go off and wander in the woods i would just start walking and before i knew it i was walking for hours and for days and then when we moved to toronto i would do it for hours until i was old enough to leave and go off on my own and then i just left without telling anyone. i joined the army i became an airborne scout where going off on my own was my job and then university and then finally and only then i came back home to visit and then disappeared and came back and that became what i did i disappeared for years maybe more than a decade and it became easier to stay away and i became afraid to find out you were dead but shawn found me somehow and isaac told me that you were going to die soon and though i did not deserve the chance to say goodbye after all that time isaac and shawn gave me that gift and i went. isaac was living in oshawa then and you were so small were you always so small but after all those years and you being sick you seemed so very small to me and your mind was not completely there but isaac closed the door to your room and i told you how much you meant to me or at least i tried because i am not sure even i do not fully understand what you were to me and i do not know that you could understand me your mind was so far gone. i like to think you understood at least enough of it that i said it to you the important parts maybe you did maybe you didn't and now putting down in words that you mattered so much and without you i would not be alive and i would not be sane and i would be in prison for murder as so many people predicted when i was young and maybe it is not politically correct to say that a white man saved me a white man who was raised to be a racist and ended up with two half indian children and then whose favourite son married a black woman and had two half black grandchildren and you struggled with what you were raised to believe and what you felt in your heart maybe today people would not say you could be a good man but you were a good man you were the only truly good man i knew as a child you are what i think of when i think of a good man and it does not matter the colour of your skin and it does not matter what you believed or what you were taught to believe but what you did and what you did was stay and be there and make sure that your children who none of us were your children were taken care of even when at times our mother tried to kill us and kill you and when two of us would not take your name you were the only thing that was solid and sure and good in our world and that is what a good father is and i thank you for that i love you for that and i will always love you for that.

you were my father.

you are my father.

i will always love you for that.

you showed me what a man is supposed to be.

not perfect.

not who i or others wanted you to be.

steadfast and present.

those seem like such simple things.

those seem like such small things. but you father were not a small thing you are no small thing. a good father is no small thing.

of all things i should know that.

you were my real father.

i may not have known how to be a son.

but somehow you still managed to be my father. somehow you managed to be a father to all of us. i wish i had time to say all of this to you when you were alive.

perhaps you are hearing this now.

and you know that you are and will always be my father.

thok ní:kon

thok ní:kon

that's it. that's all.

that's my life so far.

there are so many people that i left out so many names that i merely mentioned who deserved so much more. so many stories left untold how do you encompass a life. how do you encompass all the lives that my life came in contact with and was affected by and had an effect on. so many people worry about mattering but i look back and i'm horrified by how much i mattered even though i tried so hard or thought i tried perhaps i lied to myself maybe like all human beings i wanted to matter and i still want to matter isn't that why i'm writing these words but i look back and all the damage all the hurt despite telling myself i would not be like jack or my mother and my conviction that i would not live long enough to do much harm like a russian monk i refused to die like george chuvalo i refused to take even a knee.

and now here i am surrounded by wreckage and the summation of my life. beyond the damage that i have done is that i have seen and that i have survived.

and i am still trying to learn.

i never expected to live to get this old.

i wake up so many days in so much pain that i cannot move and i have lived a life of pain it has been my companion and then some days i wake with the black dog on my chest so large and so heavy that i cannot rise i cannot get the massive black dog off my chest and his teeth sunk deep into my bones and yet this this is more so much more it is all that pain of my life added up and more and i do not say this because i feel sorry for myself but because my way of dealing with things has been to get angry and to do something even if it was wrong even if it was driven by the asperger's that's what we called it then and the dyslexia the anger was an energy it was my driving force it gave me something to at least walk at the very least walk and some days i cannot even stand me who could never stay down or even take a knee cannot even rise and then some days i wake with the black dog on my chest so heavy that i cannot rise i cannot even summon the energy to be angry the very thing that has energized me my entire life i cannot get the black dog off my chest or loosen his foaming teeth from my bones and i tell myself that this too shall pass but some day maybe it will not and i would spit on the man that i have become. on those days that i live from the kindness of others and i despise myself for needing that kindness. me who has rarely needed or gotten the kindness of others and those few those remarkable few that have shown me kindness and love some whose names i have not even mentioned some who i have not even remembered got so little in return except what i had which was hurt and hate and pain and all that damage that wreckage that i carried with me and carry with me and i hear again that the past is in the past but it is what we are made of it is all we are made of and did not know what to do with kindness with love.

i still do not know what to do with kindness or love.

i am so familiar with hurt and pain and hate that i find comfort i snarl at familiarity like a dog that has been kicked so often that all it knows is how to be kicked or that is my excuse as it was jack's or my mother's excuse and it goes back to the

schools and the churches perhaps even before that i promised when i was young i promised myself that i would not be
them be jack or my mother or fernand and i did not do what
they did but i did harm to those who did not deserve harm. i
bit the hands that tried to feed me i answered kindness with
hate i answered love with hate no not hate worse than hate
neglect i made them think it was their fault that i walked
away when that was my answer to everything and now i cannot even stand to walk away most days and what is there left
but to look back at so many sorrows and perhaps to tell the
story so that it does get repeated again and again seeming
like a different story but always the same story that started so
long ago that nobody remembers when it was started or who
first started it or why but we keep living it again and again not
knowing why. we tell stories by repeating and repeating them
because in the end that is what we do with our lives repeating
them again and again and not knowing or recognizing that
we are repeating them because we are so good at disguising
at lying to ourselves that this is different but it is no different
until we arrive at a place that there is nothing left to repeat
or no ability to repeat it and we are left i am left with nothing
but who i am and what i have done and what i have learned
from my long life.

i heard a crow before i was born.

i heard tsó:ka'we call out before i was born.

she was telling me. warning me. that my life was going to be
a journey. a battle. and she was going to be beside me all the
way.

and before we are born we all have wings before we are born
we all can fly.

i lost my wings.

probably before i was born.

probably when my mother was pregnant with me and jack
tried to kill me by stomping on her belly. that was probably
when tsó:ka'we called me to fly away with her. to keep my
wings forever. but i didn't answer her call and i lost my wings.
there have been times when i have heard crow call me again.

there have been many times but i was stubborn i am stubborn
i have feet of clay i have never been afraid of death.

how could it possibly be worse than the life that i started out
living.

the life that i carried with me for so many years because i did
not know how to put it down.

how can you fly when you are weighed down by such a thing.

i have never been good at living.

and yet i have managed to do a lot of it.

tsó:ka'we has called me so often that her voice has grown
tired.

i have not been a good man.

and i lacked the conviction to be a truly bad man.

perhaps if i had answered tsó:ka'we's call even once.

or the call of other winged things.

perhaps i should have heard the message from some four
legged creature the bear the ohkwá:ri that was my tóta's clan
and that i met in the woods when i was just a little boy and
that let me live and that my friend roger gave himself to when
it was his time and was the mightiest thing that i have ever
known or the nikakwaho'tà:'a the coyote that i so loved as
a boy and that once took my shoe because she wanted it so
that i gave it to her and limped back on the railroad tracks
my foot all bruised but my heart filled with laughter because
every time that i saw her after that she had that shoe being

nikakwaho'tà:'a the crazy trickster must be the most fun of all always roaming and making trouble and howling at the moon but i never knew how to have that much fun only how to pretend how to have that much fun and though i swore never to be prey i could never walk the earth with the sureness of ohkwá:ri i was always looking over my shoulder i was always the hunted though i never knew by what or who i knew if i stood still for too long whatever or whoever it was would find me and so i moved i constantly moved gathering no moss or dust or rust of any kind or any living thing and tsó:ka'we called me again and again but i did not heed her call and i grew older but not wiser or better because i did not want to be here i did not want to be anywhere but still i kept walking on and on with my feet of clay until even my body refused to move anymore and i could not stay ahead of the black dog or anything or anyone else and all that was left was to look back because i stopped hearing crow call me i have not heard her voice for ages perhaps she is gone or forgotten about me or her wings have faded and withered through and nothing is left but dust and ashes.

there were many events in my life. i have lived an eventful life though i certainly did not intend to do so. when you are not attached to anything you can drift from event to event. in fact many people would say that some events in my life can only happen in fiction. things like that don't happen in real life. that's what i always joked the title of my life story would be. that can't be happening. i come from a family of killers and psychopaths and criminals on both sides so much that it seemed normal when the police showed up looking for jack or someone else in the family. i did not become a criminal but i joined the army and learned how to jump out of planes and shoot people to be good at a different kind of violence and then i was the only one in my family to go to university and then i went to los angeles to become a rock

star and studied acting and was offered a plum role on a soap
opera but i turned it down because i wanted to be a serious
actor but all i ended up doing was small plays some of which
i wrote and shakespeare and sam shepard who i learned
from by trying to speak their words and act in some small
and horrible films and i wrote and wrote but did nothing at
all with it and at one point i found myself living with roger
on the salt river reservation in arizona and got in many car
accidents one of which almost killed me and should have left
me crippled and still i wrote but kept it oh so tightly to myself
because my writing of all the things that i did and i did so
many my writing mattered because my writing was me all of
me poured out in words and i could not expose my very soul
my spirit to anyone else. i was a fighter and a martial artist
and a wrestler and i was very good and i never lost and if i
had committed to any one of them maybe i could have made
money and did something but i drifted back and forth as i
did with everything else i changed shapes and i drifted and
i became a trainer and coach and bodyguard and bouncer in
some of the toughest bars always drifting from one thing to
another never doing just one thing at a time.

and there were so many women and so many friends that i
just drifted away from.

and all these events and people were not my life were not
a life they were things that happened while i was drifting
between lives. a real life is not made up of events but of
connections and i ran as fast as i could from connection. i
was a shape shifter drifting from one event to another and
to the next event and that i told others and myself was a life.

if tsó:ka'we called out i did not hear her. perhaps i did not
want to hear her i did not want to think about a time when
i had wings a time when perhaps i was a pure thing a time
when perhaps i was alive even if i did not know what that

meant really and truly alive. and now i am broken. i am shattered. i can take no shape at all because inside or outside works well enough to do anything except look back and know i have managed to survive all of this time and not really live a life. there were many events. many people would mistake it for quite the life. but i could do so much because i did not care i could be part of so much because i drifted and never took a shape that was true that was my own. i have survived but i did not live.

i heard tsó:ka'we often but i did not listen.

i once knew how to listen but i forgot.

i am trying to learn how to listen again. not just to tsó:ka'we but to the entire world. i am trying very hard to connect. to other people. to the ones that are still here. to the earth. to katsi'tsáhere. i once knew how to connect to katsi'tsáhere. i was taught to know her in my bones and with my skin with my heart. to all the many creatures that are carried on turtle on a'nó:wara's back. i used to know them with my bones and my skin and my heart. to the trees and the plants and the fungus the cooling healing moss that grow on a'nó:wara's back. i used to know them too with my bones and my skin and my heart. i used to know that i was a part of all of this. i used to know that i was connected to all of this.

maybe that was what crow was trying to tell me.

that wings are not meant to be above it all but to see it all see it in its entirety for everything is beautiful. everyone is beautiful when you see them as their entirety in their entirety and to know it all how beautiful it is even when it is difficult even when it is breaking you the world is so beautiful life is so beautiful all of the connections are so very beautiful.

that is a small little miracle. that light that has always been there.

all i had to do was look.

and see the beauty of it all.

if we do not see the connections if we do not feel the connections then it all seems to be so brutal and so pointless and ugly.

but if we connect.

ah. if we connect.

if we connect we have wings.

if we connect we can fly.

if we connect then in the end everything is beautiful.

yes that is what tsó:ka'we has been trying to tell me from the very beginning.

i heard tsó:ka'we call to me before i was born.

i heard but i did not listen.

i am ready to listen now.

and so many others can hear her too.

perhaps they will hear me and listen too.

listen with their bones.

listen with their skin.

listen with the hearts.

just listen.

just stop.

and listen.

just listen.

and know those small miracles.

perhaps i shall hear tsó:ka'we's voice again.

i am listening.

i am listening.

and i will keep listening.

thok ní:kon

Acknowledgements

I am beholden to many people for this effort. I wish to thank Dr. Norma Dunning, who, as well as being a great writer, a truly great writer, has been my mentor, my friend, and my support in all of my writing. It was Dr. Dunning who taught me that it is good to venture into the darkness, but you must find places and times to bend towards the light. I obviously quote and make use of many of my favourite writers including Shakespeare, Faulkner—often Faulkner. The writers of the Bible, which, no matter what we decide to believe of it, is one of the greatest of all books, as Blake called it: The Great Code of Western Literature. I am also and perhaps most of all greatly beholden to my tóta and so many Aunties and other Indigenous storytellers who taught me how to tell a story in that beautiful Indigenous way. And a deep thank you to Mitchell Mittelstaed and the entire Kanien'kehá:ka class who taught me Kanien'kehá and was so very patient with this clumsy and slow to learn old student who often held up his class, and yet he nor anyone in the class ever gave me the feeling that they wanted to kill me. Niawen'kó:wa Mitchell and all the others. I've used so many of the words that you taught me.

I am grateful to my family and all the people in this story who allowed me to tell my story, including those who perhaps do not come out well. I am telling my side of the story. From my point of view. I am only showing the small amount of them that I see or saw, and there is so much more beneath the waves. Thank you. Thank you all. Without you I would not be me and this work, whatever it might be, would not exist.

Jules Delorme is a neurodivergent Kanien'kehá:ka (Mohawk) author who grew up on the Akwesasne Reserve near Cornwall, Ontario. He is of Kanien'kehá:ka and French heritage. When Delorme was twelve, his abusive parents moved the family to Toronto, where he continued to suffer bullying and abuse at home and at school.

He is the author of *faller* and *Ahshiá:ton* (*You Should Write It*), a collection of stories based on Kanien'kehá:ka oral traditions and teachings. *i heard a crow before i was born* is Delorme's third book. He lives in Toronto.

Photo: Aiden Chou